WESTENDERS

VS

EASTENDERS

WESTENDERS START HERE

First published 2008
by Black & White Publishing Ltd
29 Ocean Drive, Edinburgh EH6 6JL

1 3 5 7 9 10 8 6 4 2   08 09 10 11 12

ISBN   978 1 84502 238 9

A CIP catalogue record for this book is available from the British Library.

Typeset by RefineCatch Ltd, Bungay, Suffolk
Printed and bound by Norhaven A/S, Denmark

INTRODUCTION

Why does an EastEnder not stare out of the window in the morning?

So he'll have something to do in the afternoon.

Why don't Blackhill parents let their sons and daughters marry folk from Shettleston?

Because the kids will be too lazy to steal.

What's got one eye and smells of pish?

Blackhill.

These are the sort of questions that folk in the leafy suburban academia of the West End ask each other over their champagne mojitos, along with the kind of question designed to make the East End listener feel small and unsure of his or her place in the universe. Like:

"Do you want people to accept you as you are or do you want them to like you?"

People in the West are reacting to the suggestion that the Commonwealth Games is being shared by the city. "Shared is it? Aye, the East End is getting it and we're paying for it."

Here are the tales of the good, the bad and the ugly, and that is just the Celtic attack. No, the good, the bad and the ugly are as follows, and they do happen in the East End.

Good. Your daughter got a new job.

Bad. As a hooker.

Ugly. Your neighbours are her best clients.

Really ugly. She makes more money than you do.

This is how the WestEnders see the East. No stars rising there, no wise men, just work-shy junkies with an attitude problem and bad breath, but a shared sense of humour means that everything is just hunky-dory. "Aye, right", as we say in Glasgow when we mean "Fuck off".

These are the hits (and misses), the tales tall, true and tautological, that make the West End laugh.

1

EASTENDERS. CAN'T LIVE WITH THEM, CAN LIVE WITHOUT THEM.

In a recent survey EastEnders have proved to be the most likely to have had sex in the shower.

In the survey, carried out for a leading toiletries firm, 86% of EastEnders said that they have enjoyed sex in the shower.

The other 14% said they hadn't even been to prison yet.

While Calderpark Zoo was still open, it acquired a very rare species of gorilla. Within a few weeks the gorilla, a female, became very difficult to handle.

Upon examination, the vet determined the problem. The gorilla was in season. To make matters worse, there was no male gorilla available.

Thinking about their problem, the zookeeper thought of Pat McKay, a local lad who was the part-time worker responsible for cleaning the animal cages.

Pat, like many EastEnders, had little sense but possessed ample ability to satisfy a female of any species. The zookeeper thought they might have a solution. Pat was approached with a proposition. Would he be willing to mate with the gorilla for £500?

Pat showed some interest, but said he would have to think the matter over carefully.

The following day, he announced that he would accept their offer, but only under four conditions.

"First," Pat said, "Ah'm no gonny kiss her on the lips." The keeper quickly agreed to this condition.

"Second," he said, "ye can tell naebody aboot this, ever." The keeper again readily agreed to this.

"Third," Pat said, "I want all the weans raised as Cellik fans." Once again it was agreed.

"And last of all," Pat stated, "you're gonny huv tae gie me another week to come up with the £500."

If you saw an East End lawyer drowning in the Clyde, would you go to lunch or to a movie?

What French guy do you get when you toss a hand-grenade into an East End kitchen?

Linoleum Blownapart.

A train hits a bus filled with East End schoolgirls and they all perish.

They are in heaven trying to enter the pearly gates

when St Peter asks the first girl, "Tiffany-Jane, have you ever had any contact with a male organ?"

She giggles and shyly replies, "Well, I once touched the head of one with the tip of my finger."

St Peter says, "Okay, dip the tip of your finger in the Holy Water and pass through the gate."

St. Peter asks the next girl the same question, "Marie Therese, have you ever had any contact with a male organ?"

The girl is a little reluctant but replies, "Well, once I fondled and stroked one."

St. Peter says, "All right, dip your whole hand in the Holy Water and pass through the gate."

All of a sudden, there is a commotion in the line of girls. One girl is pushing her way to the front of the queue. When she reaches the front, St Peter says, "Bernadette, what seems to be the rush?"

The girl replies, "If I'm going to have to gargle that Holy Water, I want to do it before Jessica sticks her arse in it."

A Garngad carpet installer decides to take a cigarette break after completing the installation in the first of several rooms in the Milngavie mansion he has to do. They are not in his pocket so he begins searching, only to notice a small lump in his recently completed carpet installation. Not wanting to rip up all that work for a packet of fags he simply walks over with his lump hammer and pounds the lump flat. He decides to forgo the break and continues on to the other rooms to be carpeted.

At the end of the day he's completed his work and is loading his tools into his van when two events occur almost simultaneously. He spies his packet of cigarettes on the dashboard of the van, and the lady of the house calls out, "Excuse me, have you seen my budgie?"

Boaby and Davy fae the Calton are Siamese twins, who go to France. An on-duty gendarme spots their hired car approaching the Champs Elysees with a rear light broken. He beckons the driver to pull over, which he does and winds his window down.

The officer has a good look inside the car and notices that the driver and passenger are conjoined twins, Boaby & Davy. Instead of making an issue over the light out situation he begins to engage in some friendly chat.

Gendarme: "Ah, you are on holiday my friends?"

Davy: "Aye, that's right big yin. We've been coming every September weekend for the last 9 years."

Gendarme: "So you come to France to get away from ze rainy weather you have in Ecosse?"

Davy: "Naw, it nearly always pishes doon when we

come here. Your weather's nae better than oors, in't that right Boaby?"

Boaby: "Aye."

Gendarme: "Zen I take it you are here to enjoy our delicious French food – very healthy."

Davy: "Naw, yer food's mingin', big man, everything reeks of garlic. We've brought a box full of pieces to avoid eating your crap."

Gendarme: "Zen you must be here to drink our famous wines and cognac, surely?"

Davy: "Yer swally's boggin', we've hid tae bring a kerry oot. In't that right Boaby?"

Boaby: "Aye."

Gendarme (by now ever so slightly bemused): "Well in that case you must be here to see the Parisienne madamoiselles, ze most beautiful women in Europe."

Davy: "Yer kiddin in't ye? The burds here are dugs, ah widnae touch them wae yours."

Gendarme (by now rather irate): "Zen why do you people come to our country if everysing ees so bad?"

Boaby: "It's the only chance oor Davy gets tae drive!"

A blonde walks into a chemists in Alexandra Parade and asks the assistant for some rectum deodorant.

The pharmacist, a little bemused, explains to the woman that they don't sell rectum deodorant and never have.

The blonde assures the pharmacist that she has been buying the stuff from this shop on a regular basis and would like some more.

"I'm sorry," says the chemist. "We don't have any."

"But I always buy it here," says the blonde.

"Do you have the container that it came in?" asks the pharmacist.

"Yes," says the blonde, "I'll go home and get it."

She returns with the container and hands it to the pharmacist who looks at it and says to her, "This is just a normal stick of underarm deodorant."

Annoyed, the blonde snatches the container back and reads out loud from the container. "To apply, push up bottom."

A new report from Caledonian University suggests that being overweight in the East End is not as harmful as is commonly believed, and actually confers some surprising benefits.

Being five to ten pounds overweight could protect people from ailments ranging from tuberculosis to Alzheimer's disease, research indicates. Those carrying 15 to 25 extra pounds are better able to recover from adverse conditions such as emphysema, pneumonia and various injuries and infections, states the report.

Thirty to forty pounds of flab could help fend off breast, kidney, pancreatic, prostate, and colon cancer. And an extra fifty pounds on the scale may improve eyesight, reverse baldness, cure the common cold and reduce global warming.

In general, the report concludes, overweight people are happier, more successful in business, cleverer and friendlier.

The study was funded by a research grant from McDonald's, Burger King, Domino's Pizza, Starbucks, Häagen-Dazs and Danny's Delicious Doughnuts.

A cab picks up a nun in Byres Road. She gets into the cab, and notices that the very handsome cab driver won't stop staring at her. She asks him why he is staring. He replies, "I have a question to ask you but I don't want to offend you."

She answers, "My son, you cannot offend me. When you're as old as I am and have been a nun as long as I have, you get a chance to see and hear just about everything. I'm sure that there's nothing you could say or ask that I would find offensive."

The taxi driver says, "Well, I've always had a fantasy to have a nun kiss me."

She responds, "Let's see what we can do about that. Number one, you have to be single and number two, you must be Catholic."

The cab driver is very excited and says, "Yes, I'm single and Catholic."

"OK," the nun says. "Pull into the next side street."

The nun fulfils his fantasy, with a kiss that would make a hooker blush, but when they get back on the road the cab driver starts crying.

"My dear child," says the nun, "why are you crying?"

"Forgive me but I've sinned. I lied and I must confess. I'm married and I'm a Proddy."

The nun says, "That's OK. My name's Kevin and I'm going to a fancy dress party."

As my mate Calum, a well-known West End boulevardier, has said, "In wine there is wisdom, in beer there is freedom, in water there is bacteria."

In a number of carefully controlled trials, scientists at the Western Infirmary have demonstrated that if we drank 1 litre of water each day, at the end of the year we would have absorbed more than 1 kilo of Escherichia coli, (E. coli) – bacteria found in faeces.

In other words, we are consuming a kilo of crap.

However, we do not run that risk when drinking wine and beer (or whisky, tequila, rum, or other alcohol) because alcohol has to go through a purification process of boiling, filtering and/or fermenting.

Remember. Water = Crap, Wine = Health.

Therefore, it's better to drink wine and talk shite, than to drink water and be full of shit.

East End New Year Resolutions.

1. Read less.
2. I want to gain weight. Put on at least three stones.
3. Stop exercising. Waste of time.
4. Watch more TV. I've been missing some good stuff.
5. Procrastinate more. Or put it off.
6. Drink. Lots and lots.
7. Start being superstitious.
8. Spend less time at work.
9. Stop bringing lunch from home. I should eat out more.
10. Take up a new habit. Maybe smoking.

A woman and a baby were in the East End doctor's examining room, waiting for the doctor to come in for the baby's first exam. A young, good-looking doctor arrived, and examined the baby, checked his weight and, being a little concerned, asked if the baby was breast-fed or bottle-fed?

"Breast-fed," she replied.

"Well, strip down to your waist," the doctor ordered.

She did. He pinched her, pressed, kneaded and rubbed both breasts for a while in a very professional and detailed doctorly examination – frowning as he did so. Motioning to her to get dressed he said, "No wonder this baby is a little underweight. You don't have any milk."

"I know," she said. "I'm his granny, but I'm glad I came."

St Jude's Xmas panto for paranoid schizophrenics ended in chaos last night, when someone shouted:

"HE'S BEHIND YOU"

2

POETRY CORNER

West End Ladies' Poem

Before I lay me down to sleep,
I pray for a man, who's not a creep,
One who's handsome, smart and strong.
One who loves to listen long,
One who thinks before he speaks,
One who'll ring, not wait for weeks.
I pray he's gainfully employed,
When I spend his dosh, won't be annoyed.
Pulls out my chair and opens my door,
Massages my back and begs to do more.
Oh! Send me a man who'll make love to my mind,
Knows what to answer to 'how big is my behind?'
One who'll make love till my body's itchin',
And brings ME a sandwich too
When he goes to the kitchen.
I pray that this man will love me no end,
And never compare me to my best friend.
Thank you in advance and now I'll just wait,
For I know you will send him before it's too late.

East End Ladies Poem

He didn't like my casserole
And he didn't like my cake.
He said my biscuits were too hard . . .
Not like his mother used to make.

I didn't make the coffee right
He didn't like the stew,
I didn't mend his socks
The way his mother used to do.

I pondered for an answer
I was looking for a clue.
Then I kicked the shit out of him.

A West End Poem. The Perfect Man

The perfect man is gentle
Never cruel or mean
He has a beautiful smile
And he keeps his face so clean.

The perfect man likes children
And will raise them by your side
He will be a good father
As well as a good husband to his bride.

The perfect man loves cooking
Cleaning and vacuuming too
He'll do anything in his power
To convey his feelings of love for you.

The perfect man is sweet
Making poetry from your name
He's a best friend to your mother
And kisses away your pain.

He has never made you cry
Or hurt you in any way
Oh, fuck this stupid poem
The perfect man is gay.

An East End Love Poem

Of course I love ye darling
You're a crackin' top notch burd
And when I say you're gorgeous
I mean every single word

So yer bum is on the big side
I don't mind a bit of flab
It means that when I'm ready
There's somethin' there to grab

So your belly isn't flat no more
I tell ye, I don't care
So long as when I cuddle ye
I can get my arms round there

No woman who is your age
Has nice round perky breasts
They just gave in to gravity
But I know ye did yer best

I'm tellin' ye the truth now
I never tell ye lies
I think it's very sexy
That you've got dimples on yer thighs

I swear on ma granny's grave now
The moment that we met
I thought ye were as good as
I was ever gonny get

No matter whit ye look like
I'll always love ye dear
Now shut up while the fitba's on
And get me another beer.

East End Guy's Free Verse

I pray for a deaf-mute nymphomaniac with huge boobs who owns a pub and two seats in the Directors' Box at Parkhead.
This doesn't rhyme and I don't give a fuck.

3

OLD FOLKS' CORNER

Last night my wife and I were sitting in our kitchen in North Kelvinside and I said to her, "I never want to live in a vegetative state, dependent on some machine and fluids from a bottle to keep me alive. That would be no quality of life at all. If that ever happens, just pull the plug."

So she got up, unplugged the computer, and threw out my whisky.

Bitch.

The family wheeled Grandma, whose husband, long dead, had made a fortune out of haulage in the East End, out on to the lawn, in her wheelchair, where the activities for her 100th birthday were taking place. Grandma couldn't speak very well, but she could write notes when she needed to communicate. After a short time out on the lawn, Grandma started leaning to the right, so some family members, all educated by her and her husband's money, and mostly living in expectation in the West End, grabbed her, straightened her up, and stuffed pillows on her right.

A short time later, she started leaning off to her left, so again the family grabbed her and stuffed pillows on her left.

Soon she started leaning forward, so the family members again grabbed her, then tied a pillowcase around her waist to hold her up.

A great-grandson who arrived late came running up to Grandma and said, "Hi Great Gran, you're looking great, Gran. How are these jackals treating you?"

Grandma took out her little notepad and slowly wrote a note to the boy. "They won't let me fart."

A family in Blackhill was considering putting their grandfather in a nursing home. All of the local facilities were completely full, so they had to put him in a Masonic home in Hillhead.

After a few weeks in the Masonic home, they came to visit grandpa.

"How do you like it here?" asks the grandson.

"It's wonderful! Everyone here is so courteous and respectful," says grandpa.

"We're so happy for you. We were worried that this was the wrong place for you. You know, since you are a little different from everyone else."

"Och, no! Let me tell you about how wonderfully they treat the residents here," grandpa says with a big smile.

"There's a musician here. He's 85 years old. He hasn't played the violin in 20 years and everyone still calls him 'Maestro'.

"There is a judge in here – he's 95 years old. He hasn't been on the bench in 30 years and everyone still calls him 'Your Honour'.

"And there's a doctor here – 90 years old. He hasn't been practicing medicine for 25 years and everyone still calls him 'Doctor'!"

"And what about you, Grandpa?" asks the grandson.

"And me . . . I haven't had sex for 25 years and they still call me 'The Fucking Catholic'."

A recent study by Caledonian University claims that elderly East End people who drink beer or wine at least four times a week have the highest bone density.

The report goes on to say that they need that extra bone density, as they are the ones falling down the most.

Two 90-year-old West End women, Rose and Barbara, had been friends all of their lives. When it was clear that Rose was dying, Barbara visited her every day. One day Barbara said, "Rose, we both loved playing tennis all our lives, and we played all through school. Please do me one favour. When you get to Heaven, somehow you must let me know if there's tennis there."

Rose looked up at Barbara from her deathbed and said, "Barbara, you've been my best friend for many years. If it's at all possible, I'll do this favour for you."

Shortly after that, Rose died. At midnight a few nights later, Barbara was awakened from a sound sleep by a blinding flash of white light and a voice calling out to her, "Barbara, Barbara."

"Who is it?" asked Barbara, sitting up suddenly. "Who is it?"

"Barbara – it's me, Rose."

"You're not Rose. Rose just died."

"I'm telling you, it's me, Rose," insisted the voice.

"Rose! Where are you?"

"In Heaven," replied Rose. "I have some really good news and a little bad news."

"Tell me the good news first," said Barbara.

"The good news," Rose said, "is that there's tennis in Heaven. Better yet, all of our old pals who died before us are here, too. Better than that, we're all young again. Better still, it's always springtime, and it never rains or snows. And best of all, we can play tennis all we want and we never get tired."

"That's fantastic," said Barbara. "It's beyond my wildest dreams! So what's the bad news?"

"You're playing on Tuesday."

An elderly couple were about to get married. He's from the East, she's from the West. She said, "I want to keep my house."

He said, "That's fine with me."

She said, "And I want to keep my Mercedes."

He said, "That's fine with me."

She said, "And I want to have sex 6 times a week."

He said, "That's fine with me. Put me down for Friday."

An elderly West End couple had dinner at another couple's house and, after eating, the wives left the table and went into the kitchen. The two elderly gentlemen were talking, and one said, "Last night we went out to a new restaurant, and it was really excellent. I would recommend it very highly."

The other man said, "What is the name of the restaurant?"

The first man thought and thought and finally said, "What is the name of that flower you give to someone you love? You know, the one that is red and has thorns."

"Do you mean a rose?"

"Yes," the man said and then he turned toward the kitchen and yelled, "Rose, what's the name of that restaurant we went to last night?"

Working people frequently ask retired people what they do to make their days interesting.

Me, I went to Somerfield in Byres Road the other day. I was only in there for about 5 minutes but when I came out to go across the road to Oran Mor for a beer there was a yellow peril writing out a parking ticket, so I went up to him and said, "Come on, pal, how about giving an old guy a break?"

He ignored me and continued writing. I called him a Nazi. He glared at me and started writing another for having worn tyres. So I called him a shite. He finished the second ticket and put it on the windscreen with the first. Then he started writing a third and fourth ticket for further faults he kept finding.

This went on for about 20 minutes. The more I abused him, the more tickets he wrote.

I didn't give a monkey's, because my car was upstairs in the car park.

Real Radio was interviewing a 70-year-old West End woman, one of the first rock 'n' rollers, because she had just got married for the fourth time. The interviewer asked her questions about her life, about what it felt like to be marrying again at 70, and then about her new husband's occupation.

"He's a funeral director," she answered.

"Interesting," the interviewer thought.

He then asked her if she wouldn't mind telling him a little about her first three husbands and what they did for a living.

She paused for a few moments, needing time to reflect on all those years. After a short time, a smile came to her face and she answered proudly, explaining that she'd first married a stockbroker when she was in her early 20s, then a circus ringmaster when in her 40s, later on a minister when in her 60s, and now in her 70s, a funeral director.

The interviewer looked at her, quite astonished, and asked why she had married four men with such diverse careers.

She smiled and explained, "It was one for the money, two for the show, three to get ready, then go, cat, go."

At a Senior Citizen's dinner in the West End, an elderly gentleman and an elderly woman struck up a conversation and discovered that they both loved to fish. Since both of them were widowed, they decided to go fishing together the next day.

The gentleman picked the lady up, and they headed to the river to his fishing boat and started out on their adventure. They carried on until they came to a fork in the river, and the gentleman asked the lady, "Do you want to go up or down?" All of a sudden the lady stripped off her clothes and made mad passionate love to the man. When they finished, the man couldn't believe what had just happened, but he had just experienced the best sex that he'd had in years.

They fished for a while and continued on down the river, when soon they came upon another fork in the river. He again asked the lady, "Up or down?" There she went again, stripped off her clothes, and made wild passionate love to him again.

This really impressed the elderly gentleman, so he asked her to go fishing again the next day. She said yes and there they were the next day, riding in the boat when they came upon the fork in the river, and the elderly gentleman asked, "Up or down?"

The woman replied, "Down."

A little puzzled and disappointed, the gentleman guided the boat down the river when he came upon another fork in the river and he asked the woman, "Up or down?"

She replied, "Up."

This really confused the man so he asked, "What's the score here? Yesterday, every time I asked you if you wanted to go up or down you made mad passionate love to me. Now today, nothing."

She replied, "Well, yesterday I wasn't wearing my

hearing aid and I thought that the choices were fuck or drown."

An East End octogenarian, who was an avid golfer, moved to the West and joined the local club. He went to the club for the first time to play, but he was told there wasn't anyone with whom he could play because they were already out on the course. He repeated several times that he really wanted to play. Finally, the assistant pro said he would play with him and asked how many strokes he wanted for a bet. The 80-year-old said, "I really don't need any strokes because I have been playing quite well. The only real problem I have is getting out of bunkers."

And he did play well. Coming to the par four eighteenth they were even. The pro had a nice drive and was able to get on the green and a two-putt for a par. The old man had a good drive, but his approach shot landed in a bunker next to the green. Playing from the bunker, he hit a high ball which landed on the green and rolled into the hole. Birdie, match and all the money, ya dancer. The pro walked over to the bunker where his opponent was still standing.

He said, "Nice shot, but I thought you said you have a problem getting out of bunkers?"

Replied the octogenarian, "I do. Please give me a hand."

EastEnders have much shorter life spans than do WestEnders and the whole of the West End is getting to look like a retirement home. Here are a few tips that will tell you how to recognize how much you have aged.

The Botanic Gardens has a bench with your name on it ready.

When your doctor doesn't give you X-rays any more, but just holds you up to the light.

When you remember when the Dead Sea was only sick.

You know all the answers, but nobody asks the questions.

When your wife says. "Let's go upstairs and make love" and you answer: "I can't do both!"

Going braless pulls all the wrinkles out of your face.

When you don't care where your spouse goes, just as long as you don't have to go too.

You and your teeth don't sleep together.

Your back goes out, but you stay in.

You wake up looking like your passport picture.

Your idea of a night out is sitting on the front steps.

Happy hour is a nap.

Your idea of weightlifting is standing up.

It takes longer to rest than it did to get tired.

The twinkle in your eye is only the reflection of the sun on your bifocals.

You sit in a rocking chair and can't get it going.

You wonder how you could be over the hill when you don't even remember being on top of it.

You don't know real embarrassment until your hip sets off a metal detector.

Every time you suck in your belly, your ankles swell.

Age always corresponds inversely to the size of your multivitamin.

It's harder and harder for sexual harassment charges to stick.

Your secrets are safe with your friends because they can't remember them either.

No one expects you to run into a burning building.

There's nothing left to learn the hard way.

Your joints are more accurate than the BBC Weather Service.

You're sitting on a park bench, and a Boy Scout comes up and helps you cross your legs.

Someone compliments you on your layered look, and you're wearing a bikini.

You start videotaping daytime game shows.

Conversations with people your own age often turn into "dueling ailments".

You run out of breath walking DOWN a flight of stairs.

You look both ways before crossing a room.

You frequently find yourself telling people what a loaf USED to cost.

You realize that a stamp today costs more than a movie did when you were growing up.

Many of your co-workers were born the same year that you got your last promotion.

The clothes you've put away until they come back in style come back in style.

The car that you bought brand new becomes an antique.

You're asleep, but others worry that you're dead.

You stop trying to hold your stomach in, no matter who walks into the room.

Your best friend is dating someone half their age and isn't breaking any laws.

Your arms are almost too short to read the *Herald*.

You enjoy hearing about other people's operations.

You consider coffee one of the most important things in life.

The end of your tie doesn't come anywhere near the top of your trousers.

You know what the word 'equity' means.

Your ears are hairier than your head.

You talk about 'good grass' and you're referring to someone's lawn.

You have a party and the neighbours don't even realize it.

Everything that works hurts, and what doesn't hurt doesn't work.

You feel like the morning after, and you haven't been anywhere.

Your little black book only contains names starting with Dr.

Your knees buckle and your belt won't.

You sink your teeth into a steak, and they stay there.

Old aunties used to come up to me at weddings, poking me in the ribs and cackling, telling me, "You're next." They stopped after I started doing the same thing to them at funerals.

4

SUFFER THE LITTLE CHILDREN

A Hillhead father asked his 10-year-old son if he knew about the birds and the bees.

"I don't want to know," the child said, bursting into tears. "Promise me you won't tell me."

Confused, the father asked what was wrong.

The boy sobbed, "When I was six, I got the 'There's no Easter Bunny. The Americans made it up' speech."

"At seven, I got the 'There's no Tooth Fairy' speech.

"When I was eight, you give me the 'There's no Santa' speech.

"If you're going to tell me that grown-ups don't really shag, I'll have nothing left to live for."

A three-year-old boy examined his penis and scrotum while taking a bath.

"Mum," he asked. "Are these my brains?"

"Not yet," she replied.

A North Kelvinside fireman is working outside the

station when he notices a little girl in a little red cart with wee ladders on the sides and a garden hose coiled in the middle. She is wearing a yellow plastic fireman's helmet. The cart is being pulled by her dog and her cat.

"That is a nice fire engine," the smoke eater says with admiration.

"Thanks," the girl says. The fire fighter takes a closer look and notices the girl has tied the cart to her dog's collar and to the cat's testicles. "Wee one," the fireman says, "I don't want to tell you how to run your own engine, but if you were to tie that rope around the cat's collar, I think you could go faster."

The little girl replies thoughtfully. "You're probably right, but then I wouldn't have a siren."

Two small boys, one East End Catholic and one West End Protestant, get lost in the woods. Darkness comes down and they near a monastery. Upon entering they are asked their faith, telling the head monk their religions. The Catholic lad gets the best of treatment, good food and a good bed near the fireplace. The Protestant laddie, however, gets a bowl of cold porridge and is told to sleep by the draughty door to keep the cold out of the room. In the morning the head monk asks the boys how it was.

"I dreamt I was in heaven, Father," said the Catholic boy. "It was just wonderful."

"I dreamt that I was in hell," said the Protestant boy.

"And what was that like?" asked the abbott.

"Just like this place, you couldn't get near the fire for East End Catholics."

A little West End boy goes to his dad and asks, "What is politics?" as wee West End boys do.

Dad says, "Well son, let me try to explain it this way. I am head of this family, so call me the Prime Minister. Your mother is the administrator of the money, so we'll call her the government. We are here to take care of your needs, so we will call you the people. The nanny, we will consider her as the working class and your baby brother, we will call him the future. Now think about that and see if it makes sense."

So the wee boy goes off to bed thinking about what his dad has said.

Later that night, he hears his baby brother crying, so he gets up to check on him. He finds that the baby has seriously shat his nappy. The little boy goes to his parents' room and finds his mother asleep. Not wanting to wake her up, he goes to the nanny's room, and on finding the door locked, he peeks through the keyhole and sees his father in bed with the nanny. He gives up and goes back to bed.

The next morning, the little lad says, "I think I understand the concept of politics now."

The father says, "Good, son, now tell me in your own words what you think politics is about."

The little boy replies, "The Prime Minister is screwing the working class while the government is asleep. The people are being ignored, and the future is in deep shit."

A little boy was overheard praying. "Lord, if you can't make me a better boy, don't worry about it. I'm having a really good time the way I am."

After the christening of his baby brother in church, wee Jason sobbed all the way home in the back seat of the car. His father asked him three times what was wrong. Finally, the boy replied, "That priest said he wanted us brought up in a Christian home, and I wanted to stay with you."

A Sunday school teacher asked her children as they were on the way to church service: "And why is it necessary to be quiet in church?"

One bright little girl replied, "Because people are sleeping."

A mother was preparing pancakes for her sons, Kevin, 5, and Ryan, 3.

The boys began to argue over who would get the first pancake. Their mother saw the opportunity for a moral lesson. "If Jesus were sitting here, He would say, 'Let my brother have the first pancake, I can wait.'"

Kevin turned to his younger brother and said, "Ryan, you be Jesus."

A father was at the beach with his children when the four-year-old son ran up to him, grabbed his hand and led him to the shore where a seagull lay dead in the sand. "Daddy, what happened to him?" the son asked.

"He died and went to Heaven," the Dad replied.

The boy thought a moment and then said, "Did God throw him back down?"

A wife invited some people to dinner. At the table, she turned to their six-year-old daughter and said, "Would you like to say grace?"

"I wouldn't know what to say," the girl replied.

"Just say what you hear Mummy say," the wife answered.

The daughter bowed her head and said, "Jesus, why the fuck did I invite all these people to dinner?"

Years ago, while packing for a trip, my (then) three-year-old daughter was having a wonderful time playing on the bed. At one point she said, "Daddy, look at this," and stuck out two of her fingers.

Trying to keep her entertained, I reached out and stuck her tiny fingers in my mouth and said, "Daddy's gonny eat your fingers," pretending to eat them.

I went back to packing, looked up again and my daughter was standing on the bed staring at her fingers with a devastated look on her face.

I asked, "What's wrong, darling?"

She replied: "Where's my snotter?"

The marriage of 80-year-old Diddling Dave to his 20-year-old housekeeper was the talk of the town. After being married a year, the couple went to the hospital for the birth of their first child.

The nurse came out of the delivery room to congratulate old Dave and said, "This is amazing. How do you do it at your age?"

Dave grinned and said, "You got to keep the auld motor running."

The following year, the couple returned to the hospital for the birth of their second child. The same nurse was attending the delivery and again went out to congratulate Dave. She said, "Dave, you are something else. How do you manage it?"

Dave grinned and said, "You got to keep the auld motor running."

A year later, the couple returned to the hospital for the birth of their third child.

The same nurse was there for this birth also and, after the delivery, she once again approached old Dave, smiled, and said, "Well, you really are something else. How do you do it?"

Dave replied, "It's like I've told you before, you got to keep the auld motor running."

The nurse, still smiling, patted him on the back and said, "Well, I think it might be time to change the oil. This one's black."

5

WEST END THOUGHTS

Support bacteria. They're the only culture some EastEnders have.

EastEnders are like laxatives. They irritate the shit out of you.

EastEnders are like weather. Nothing can be done to change them.

EastEnders are like insurance policies. They take soooooooo long to mature.

EastEnders are like mascara. They usually run at the first sign of emotion.

EastEnders are like lava lamps. Fun to look at, but not very bright.

Some observations.

If at first you don't succeed, skydiving is not for you.

Life is sexually transmitted.

Good health is merely the slowest possible rate at which one can die.

Men have two emotions, hungry and horny. If you see him without an erection, make him a sandwich.

Give an East End person a fish and you feed them for a day. Teach them to use the internet and they won't bother you for weeks.

Some East End people are like a Slinky. Not really good for anything, but you still can't help but smile when you shove them down the stairs.

Health freaks are going to feel stupid some day, lying in hospitals dying of nothing.

All of us could take a lesson from the weather. It pays no attention to criticism.

Why does a slight tax increase cost you £200.00 and a substantial tax cut saves you £30.00?

In the 60s, people took acid to make the world weird. Now the world is weird and people take Prozac to make it normal.

Save the whales. Collect the whole set.

42.7 percent of all statistics are made up on the spot. Not this one, though, oh no.

Over 99 percent of East End lawyers give the rest a bad name.

I feel like I'm diagonally parked in a parallel universe.

Honk if you love peace and quiet.

Remember, half the people you know are below average.

The early bird may get the worm, but the second mouse gets the cheese.

Monday is an awful way to spend 1/7 of your week.

A clear conscience is usually the sign of a bad memory.

Plan to be spontaneous tomorrow.

Always try to be modest, and be proud of it!

If you think nobody cares, try missing a couple of payments.

How many of you believe in psycho-kinesis? Raise my hand.

OK, so what's the speed of dark?

How do you tell when you're out of invisible ink?

If everything seems to be going well, you have obviously overlooked something.

When everything is coming your way, you're in the wrong lane.

If Barbie is so popular, why do you have to buy her friends?

Eagles may soar, but weasels don't get sucked into jet engines.

What happens if you get scared half to death twice?

I used to have an open mind but my brains kept falling out.

Why do psychics have to ask you for your name?

Inside every older person is a younger person wondering what the fuck happened.

Just remember – if the world didn't suck, we would all fall off.

Life in the East End isn't about how to survive the storm, but how to dance in the rain.

Golf club no women rule. That's as in no women except those under 25 with big tits.

If you can't fix it with a hammer, it's an electrical problem.

And remember.
Life is like a roll of toilet paper.
The closer it gets to the end, the faster it goes.

6

PUNNY, PUNNY, PUNNY

Three EastEnders are sitting smoking cannabis. After a few spliffs they run out of gear. One of the men stands up and says, "Look, we've got loads more tobacco, I'll just nip into the kitchen and make one of my speciality spliffs."

Off he goes into the kitchen where he takes some cumin, turmeric and a couple of other spices from the spice rack, grinds them up and rolls them into a spliff.

On his return he hands it to one of his smoking partners who lights it and takes a long puff on it. Within seconds he passes out. Ten minutes go by and he's still out cold, so they decide to take him to the Royal.

On arrival he is wheeled into Emergency. The doctor returns to his friends and asks, "So what was he doing then? Cannabis?"

"Well sort of," replies one of the guys, "but we ran out of gear, so I made a home-made spliff."

"Oh," replies the doctor, "so what did you put in it?"

"Eh, a bit of cumin, some turmeric and a couple of other spices."

The doctor sighs, "Well, that explains it."

"Why, what's wrong with him?" demands one of the men.

The doctor replies, "He's in a korma."

Far away in the tropical waters of the Caribbean, two prawns were swimming around in the sea. One is called Justin and the other is called Christian. The prawns were constantly being harassed and threatened by sharks that inhabited the area.

Finally one day Justin said to Christian, "I'm fed up with being a prawn; I wish I was a shark, and then I wouldn't have any worries about being eaten."

A large mysterious cod appeared and said, "Your wish is granted."

Lo and behold, Justin turned into a shark.

Horrified, Christian immediately swam away, afraid of being eaten by his old mate.

Time passed (as it does) and Justin found life as a shark boring and lonely. All his old mates simply swam away whenever he came close to them. Justin didn't realize that his new menacing appearance was the cause of his sad plight.

While swimming alone one day he saw the mysterious cod again and he thought perhaps the mysterious fish could change him back into a prawn.

He approached the cod and begged to be changed back, and, once again lo and behold, he found himself turned back into a prawn. With tears of joy in his tiny little eyes Justin swam back to his friends and bought them all a cocktail.

The punchline does not involve a prawn cocktail. It's much worse.

Looking around the gathering at the reef he realized he couldn't see his old pal. "Where's Christian?" he asked. "He's at home, still distraught that his best friend changed sides to the enemy and became a shark," came the reply.

Eager to put things right again and end the mutual pain and torture, he set off to Christian's abode. As he opened the coral gate, memories came flooding back. He banged on the door and shouted, "It's me, Justin, your old friend. Come out and see me again."

Christian replied, "No way ma man, you'll eat me. You're now a shark, the enemy, and I'll not be tricked into being your dinner."

Justin cried back, "No, I'm not. That was the old me. I've changed. I've found Cod. I'm a Prawn again, Christian."

Stevie Wonder is playing his first gig in the Pavilion and the place is absolutely packed to the rafters. The East End crowd is in.

In a bid to break the ice with his new audience he asks if anyone would like him to play a request. A wee toothless half-deaf old Cranhill man jumps out of his seat in the first row and shouts at the top of his voice, "Play a jazz chord! Play a jazz chord!"

Amazed that this guy knows about his varied career, the blind impresario starts to play an E minor scale and then goes into a difficult jazz melody for about 10 minutes. When he finishes the whole place goes wild.

The old man jumps up again and shouts, "No Big Man. No Stevie! No! Play a jazz chord, play a jazz chord!"

Stevie is a bit peeved by this but being the professional that he is, dives straight into a jazz improvisation with his band around the B flat minor chord and really tears the place apart. The crowd goes wild with this impromptu show of his technical expertise.

The old man jumps up again. "No! No! Play a jazz chord Stevie, play a jazz chord!"

Stevie is starting to get really annoyed now as the man doesn't seem to appreciate his playing ability.

Stevie shouts to him from the stage, "OK smartass. You get up here and do it!"

The wee old guy climbs up on to the stage, takes hold of the microphone and starts to sing.

"A jazz chord, to say, I love you!"

The Lone Ranger and Tonto walked into a saloon and sat down to have a beer. After a few minutes, a big tall cowboy walked in and asked, "Who owns the big white horse outside?" The Lone Ranger stood up, hitched his gun belt, and answered. "I do. Why?"

The cowboy looked at the Lone Ranger and replied, "I just thought you'd like to know, your horse outside is about dead."

The Lone Ranger and Tonto rushed outside and sure enough, Silver was ready to die from heat exhaustion. The Lone Ranger got the horse some water and soon Silver was starting to feel a little better.

The Lone Ranger turned to Tonto and said, "Tonto, I want you to run around Silver and see if you can create enough of a breeze to make him feel better."

Tonto said, "Sure, Kemosabe," and started running circles around Silver.

Not able to do anything else but wait, the Lone Ranger returned to the saloon to finish his beer. A few minutes later, another cowboy struts into the bar and asks, "Who owns that big white horse outside?"

The Lone Ranger stands again . . . and claims, "I do! What's wrong with him this time?"

The cowboy looks him in the eye and says, "Nothing . . . but you left your injun runnin."

7

THE GOOD, THE BAD, AND THE UGLY, WEST END STYLE

Good. Your wife is pregnant.
Bad.　It's triplets.
Ugly.　You had a vasectomy five years ago.

Good. Your wife's not talking to you.
Bad.　She wants a divorce.
Ugly.　She's a lawyer.

Good. Your son is finally maturing.
Bad.　He's involved with the woman next door.
Ugly.　So are you.

Good. Your son studies a lot in his room.
Bad.　You find several porn movies hidden there.
Ugly.　You're in them.

Good. Your hubby and you agree, no more kids.
Bad.　You can't find your birth control pills.
Ugly.　Your twelve year old daughter borrowed them.

Good. Your husband understands fashion.
Bad. He's a cross-dresser.
Ugly He looks better than you.

Good. You give the 'birds and bees' talk to your daughter.
Bad. She keeps interrupting.
Ugly. With corrections.

Good. Your son is shagging someone new.
Bad. It's another man.
Ugly. He's your best pal.

8

RAINY DAY WOMEN

A West End woman was having a daytime shag while her husband was at work. One wet and rainy day she was in bed with her boyfriend when, to her horror, she heard her husband's car outside. She looked out of the window and yelled to her lover, "Quick, jump out of the window. My husband's home early."

"I can't jump out the window! It's raining out there."

"If my husband catches us in here, he'll kill us both!" she replied. "He's from the East End and has a very quick temper plus a shotgun in the car. The rain is the least of your problems!"

So the boyfriend scrambles out of bed, grabs his clothes and jumps out the window. As he began running down Byres Road in the pouring rain, he discovered he had run right into the middle of the Glasgow Marathon. So he started running alongside the others, thousands of them. Being naked, with his clothes tucked under his arm, he tried to blend in as best he could.

After a little while, a small group of runners, who

had been studying him with some curiosity, jogged closer.

"Do you always run in the nude?" one asked.

"Oh yes," he replied, gasping in air. "It feels so wonderfully free."

Another runner moved alongside.

"Do you always run carrying your clothes with you under your arm?"

"Oh, yes," the guy answered breathlessly. "That way I can get dressed at the end of the run and get in the car to go home."

Then a third runner cast his eyes a little lower and queried, "Do you always wear a condom when you run?"

"No. Just when it's raining."

The first year Glasgow Uni student had just got an old banger as a starting present from his parents. He took it for a spin in Milngavie but misjudged the road and overturned the car directly between the house of Mr and Mrs Smith and Mr and Mrs Balls.

Luckily, he was pulled out by the Smiths.

Calum to Ian in the Doublet Bar in the West End: "I just read an article on the dangers of drinking. It scared the shit out of me. Bad breath, liver disease, brain shrinkage and lots of other stuff. So that's it. After today, no more reading."

The Archbishop of Canterbury has almost got his way. British weather has been declared Muslim.

It's partly Sunni but mostly Shi'ite.

A West End accountant was on holiday in London and every night he returned to his hotel, full of the wonders of the city. So much so that another guest asked, "Is this your first visit?"

"Aye, it is."

"You seem to be having a great time."

"Aye, I am that."

"Good."

"And what's more, it's not just a holiday. It's my honeymoon as well."

"Oh. Where's your wife?"

"Och, she's been here before."

Two Blackhill blondes, Tracy and Sharon, are talking about their boyfriends.

Tracy says, "I love my boyfriend so much but he has terrible dandruff and doesn't know what to do about it".

Sharon says, "Give him Head and Shoulders"

Tracy asks, "How do you give shoulders?"

After the collapse of Zoom, the West End is starting a new airline. They plan to dump the male flight attendants. No one wanted them in the first place. Then they will replace all the stewardesses with good-looking strippers. What the hell. They don't even serve food any more, so what's the loss?

The strippers would at least triple the alcohol sales and get a party atmosphere going in the plane. And, of course, every businessman in the country would start flying again, hoping to see naked women.

Because of the tips, the women wouldn't need a salary, thus saving even more money. The WestEnders suggest tips would be so good that they could charge the women for working on the plane and have them kick back 20%, including lap dances.

And the clincher. Terrorists would be afraid to get on the planes for fear of seeing naked women. Hijackings would come to a screeching halt, and the whole industry would see record profits.

This is definitely a win/win situation. If they handle it right, it is a golden opportunity to turn a liability into an asset. Shares are available from: I'mIanBFlyme.com

A West End hubby walks into Ann Summers to purchase some see-through lingerie for his wife. He is shown several possibilities that range from £50 to £150 in price, the more see-through, the higher the price. He opts for the sheerest item, pays the £150 and takes the lingerie home.

He presents it to his wife and asks her to go upstairs, put it on and model it for him. Upstairs, the wife thinks, "I have an idea. It's so see-through that it might as well be nothing. I'll not put it on, do the modelling naked and return it tomorrow and get a £150 refund for myself."

So she appears naked at the top of the stairs and strikes a pose.

The husband says, "Jesus! It wasn't that creased in the shop."

A man walks into the City Bakeries, slaps a £50 note on the counter and says, "A meringue?"

The girl behind the counter replies, "Aye, ye're right, but come back after 6 o'clock when the shoap's shut!"

Joe the East End gangster got himself killed. His will provided £30,000 for an elaborate funeral. As the last guests departed, his West End wife Helen turned to her oldest friend.

"Well, I'm sure Joe would be pleased," she said.

"I'm sure you're right," replied Jody, who lowered her voice and leaned in close. "How much did this really cost?"

"All of it," said Helen. "Thirty thousand."

"No!" Jody exclaimed. "I mean, it was very nice, but £30,000?"

Helen answered. "The funeral was £6,500. I donated £500 to the church. The wake, food and drink were another £500. The rest went for the stone."

Jody computed quickly. "£22,500 for a memorial stone? Jesus, how big is it?"

"Two and a half carats."

An Englishman, an EastEnder and a WestEnder were in a pub, talking about their sons. "My son was born on St George's Day," commented the Englishman. "So we obviously decided to call him George."

"That's a real coincidence," remarked the Wendie. "My son was born on St Andrew's Day, so obviously we decided to call him Andrew."

"That's incredible, what a coincidence," said the EastEnder. "Exactly the same thing happened with my son, Pancake."

An old WestEnder was boasting to his neighbour, "I've just bought a new hearing aid. It cost me four thousand pounds, but it's state of the art. It's perfect."

"Really," answered the neighbour. "What kind is it?"

"Half past twelve."

A lesson on how consultants can make a difference in an organisation. Last week, we took some friends to a new West End restaurant, Stevie's Place, and noticed that the waiter who took our order carried a spoon in his shirt pocket. It seemed a little strange. When the other waiter brought our wine and cutlery, I observed that he also had a spoon in his shirt pocket.

Then I looked around and saw that all the staff had spoons in their pockets. When the waiter came back to serve our soup I inquired, "Why the spoon?"

"Well," he explained, "the restaurant's owner hired consultants to revamp all of our processes. After several months of analysis, they concluded that the spoon was the most frequently dropped utensil. It represents a drop frequency of approximately 3 spoons per table per hour. If our personnel are better prepared, we can reduce the number of trips back to the kitchen and save 15 man hours per shift."

As luck would have it, I dropped my spoon and he replaced it with his spare. "I'll get another spoon next time I go to the kitchen instead of making an extra trip to get it now." I was impressed.

Then I noticed that there was a string hanging out

of the waiter's fly. Looking around, I saw that all of the waiters had the same string hanging from their flies. So, before he walked off, I asked the waiter, "Excuse me, but can you tell me why you have that string there?"

"Oh, certainly." Then he lowered his voice. "Not everyone is so observant. That consulting firm I mentioned also learned that we can save time in the toilet. By tying this string to the tip of our willies, we can pull it out without touching it and eliminate the need to wash our hands, shortening the time spent in the toilet by 76.39%." I asked quietly, "After you get it out, how do you put it back?"

"Well," he whispered, "I don't know about the others, but I use the spoon."

9

WURDZ

WestEnders, bored with the paucity of the words available in the Scottish and English languages, have taken to inventing their own. Here are a few examples.

PICASSO BUM
A woman whose knickers are too small for her, so that she looks as if she has four buttocks.

TESTICULATING
Waving your arms around and talking total bollocks.

BLAMESTORMING
Sitting round in a group, discussing why a deadline was missed or a project failed, and why Gordon Strachan was responsible.

SEAGULL MANAGER
A manager who flies in, makes a lot of noise, shits on everything and everybody, and then leaves.

ARSEMOSIS
The process by which people seem to absorb success and advancement by crawling up the arse of the boss rather than by working hard.

SALMON DAY
The experience of spending an entire day swimming upstream only to get fucked and die.

SITCOMs
Single Income, Two Children, Oppressive Mortgage. What yuppies turn into when they have children and one of them stops working to stay home with the kids or start a 'home business'.

SINBAD
Single income, no boyfriend and desperate.

AEROPLANE BLONDE
One who has dyed her hair but still has a 'black box'.

PERCUSSIVE MAINTENANCE
The fine art of battering the shit out of an electronic device to get it to work again.

ADMINISPHERE
The rarefied organisational layers beginning just above the rank and file. Decisions that fall from the 'adminisphere' are often profoundly inappropriate or irrelevant to the problems they were designed to solve. This is often affiliated with the dreaded 'administrivia' – needless paperwork and processes.

AW NAW SECOND
That minuscule fraction of time in which you realize that you've just made a BIG mistake (e.g. you've hit 'reply all').

GREYHOUND
A very short skirt, only an inch from the hare.

JIMMY-NO-STARS
A young man of substandard intelligence, the typical adolescent who works in a burger bar. The 'no-stars' comes from the badges displaying stars that staff at these restaurants wear to show their level of training.

MILLENNIUM DOMES
The contents of a Michelle Mone bra, i.e. extremely impressive when viewed from the outside, but there's actually nothing in there worth seeing.

MONKEY BATH

A bath so hot that, when lowering yourself in, you go, "Oo! Oo! Oo! Aa! Aa! Aa!"

MYSTERY BUS

The bus that arrives at the pub on Friday night while you're in the toilet after your 10th pint, and whisks away all the unattractive people, so the place is suddenly packed with stunners when you come back in.

MYSTERY TAXI

The taxi that arrives at your place on Saturday morning before you wake up, whisks away the stunner you slept with, and leaves a 10-pinter in your bed instead.

BEER JAIKET

The invisible but warm jacket worn when walking home after a booze cruise in January. At 3am.

BEER COMPASS

The invisible device that ensures your safe arrival home after the booze cruise, even though you're too drunk to remember where you live, how you got here, and where you've come from.

BREAKING THE SEAL

Your first pee in the pub, usually after 2 hours of drinking. After breaking the seal of your bladder, repeat visits to the toilet will be required every 10 or 15 minutes for the rest of the night.

TART FUEL

Bottled alcopoppy spirits, regularly consumed by young women.

And single words, mostly from the Western Infirmary staff.

Artery. The study of paintings

Bacteria. Back door to cafe

Barium. What doctors do when patients die

Benign. What you be, after you be eight

Caesarean Section. A place in Rome

Catscan. Searching for kitty

Cauterize. Made eye contact with her

Colic. A sheepdog

Coma. A punctuation mark

Dilate. To live long

Enema. Not a friend

Fester. Quicker than someone else

Fibula. A small lie

Impotent. Distinguished, well known

Labour Pain. Getting hurt at work

Medical Staff. A doctor's cane

Morbid. A higher offer

Nitrates. Cheaper than day rates

Node. I knew it

Outpatient. A person who has fainted

Recovery Room. Place to do upholstery

Rectum. Nearly killed him

Secretion. Hiding something

Seizure. Roman emperor

Tablet. A small table

Terminal Illness. Getting sick at the airport

Tumour. One plus one more

Urine. Opposite of you're out

10

A WUNCH OF BANKERS

A new sign in the bank reads:

"Please note that this bank is installing new drive-through ATMs, enabling customers to withdraw cash without leaving their motors. Customers using this new facility are requested to use the procedures outlined below when accessing their accounts. After months of careful research, procedures have been developed. Please follow the appropriate steps for your geographical area."

West End procedure.

1. Drive up to the cash machine.

2. Put down your car window.

3. Insert card into machine and enter PIN.

4. Enter amount of cash required and withdraw.

5. Retrieve card, cash and receipt.

6. Put window up.

7. Drive off.

East End procedure.

First, steal your car, then.

1. Drive up to cash machine.

2. Reverse and back up the required amount to align car window with the machine.

3. Pull on handbrake, put the window down.

4. Find wallet or handbag, tip all contents on to passenger seat to locate card.

5. Tell person on moby you will call them back and hang up.

6. Attempt to insert card into machine.

7. Open car door to allow easier access to machine due to its excessive distance from the car.

8. Insert card.

9. Reinsert card the right way round.

10. Dig through handbag or wallet once again to find diary with your PIN written on the inside back page.

11. Enter PIN.

12. Press cancel and re-enter correct PIN.

13. Enter amount of cash required.

14. Check queue of cars in rear view mirror. Sneer.

15. Retrieve cash and receipt.

16. Empty wallet or handbag again and place cash inside.

17. Instantly lose receipt.

18. Re-check queue of cars. Sneer.

19. Drive forward 2 feet.

20. Reverse back to cash machine.

21. Retrieve card.

22. Locate wee plastic card holder, and place card into the slot provided.

23. Give intimidating look to irate drivers waiting behind you.

24. Restart stalled engine and drive off.

25. Redial person on moby.

26. Drive for 2 or 3 miles.

27. Release handbrake.

EASTENDERS

VS

WESTENDERS

EASTENDERS START HERE

First published 2008
by Black & White Publishing Ltd
29 Ocean Drive, Edinburgh EH6 6JL

1 3 5 7 9 10 8 6 4 2   08 09 10 11 12

ISBN: 978 1 84502 238 9

A CIP catalogue record for this book is available from the British Library.

Typeset by RefineCatch Ltd, Bungay, Suffolk
Printed and bound by Norhaven A/S, Denmark

INTRODUCTION

The 28% that the people from the West End live longer than the EastEnders is all spent talking about the decline in property values, as is the other 72%, so what is the point of living longer? A bigger percentage of their kids go to private schools and universities, but most of them are so thick that you could drive nails into them without them noticing and as for any sense of fashion or style, forget it. The West End buys fashion, the East End creates it.

As for leafy suburban academia, you can stick it where the sun don't shine. EastEnders don't hide in big houses and gossip about their neighbours, they gossip about their neighbours in the streets and pubs, and if the gossip does tend to the more physical and leads to the odd stabbing in the East, at least you get stabbed in the front, rather than the mental wounds inflicted by the backstabbing, arrogant snobs of the West, most of whom are feart to go further East than the High Street without an escort of uniformed, helmeted fascists, aka the polis.

And the East End can and do laugh at themselves. St Jude's Xmas panto for paranoid schizophrenics

ended in chaos last night when someone shouted, "HE'S BEHIND YOU!" which is typical of the black humour that thrives in the East End.

Adversity and deprivation? Come ahead! The East End thrives on it. And the West End will be laughing on the other side of its face when they and the Government pay ten times the current estimate for a nice shiny new East End when they get the Commonwealth Games. And do you know the difference between Celtic and Partick Thistle? One of them wins things.

These are the jibes, jabs and gibberings that make the people of the East End the salt (and vinegar) of the earth.

1

SUFFER THE LITTLE CHILDREN

The scene is one of the West End's more expensive private schools. Wee Hughie's da, a Dennistoun man, has won the lottery and is aiming for the best for his son, he thinks.

Teacher: "Good morning children, today is Thursday, so we're going to have a general knowledge quiz. The pupil who gets the answer right can have Friday and Monday off and not come back to school until Tuesday."

Wee Hughie thinks, "Ya beauty! I'm pure dead brilliant at general knowledge, so I am. This is gonny be a doddle!"

Teacher: "Right class, who can tell me who said, 'Don't ask what your country can do for you, but what you can do for your country'?"

Wee Hughie shoots up his hand, waving furiously in the air.

Teacher, looking round, picks Farqhuar Fauntelroy at the front. "Yes, Farquhar?"

Farquhar (in a very English accent): "Yes miss, the answer is J F Kennedy – inauguration speech 1960."

Teacher: "Very good Farquhar. You may stay off Friday and Monday and we will see you back in class on Tuesday."

The next Thursday comes around, and Wee Hughie is even more determined.

Teacher: "Who said, 'We shall fight on the beaches, we shall fight on the landing grounds, we shall fight in the fields and in the streets, we shall fight in the hills; we shall never surrender'?"

Wee Hughie's hand shoots up, arm stiff as a board, shouting, "I know. I know. Me Miss, me Miss."

Teacher looks around and picks Tarquin Smythe, sitting at the front: "Yes Tarquin?"

Tarquin (in a very, very posh, English accent): "Yes miss, the answer is Winston Churchill, 1941 Battle of Britain speech."

Teacher: "Very good Tarquin, you may stay off Friday and Monday and come back to school on Tuesday."

The following Thursday comes around and Wee Hughie is hyper. He's been studying encyclopedias all week and he's ready for anything that comes. He's coiled in his wee chair, dribbling in anticipation.

Teacher: "Who said, 'One small step for man, one giant leap for mankind'?"

Wee Hughie's arm shoots straight in the air, he's standing on his seat, jumping up and down scream-

ing, "Me miss. Me miss. I know, I know. Me Miss, me miss, meeeeee."

Teacher, looking round the class, picks Rupert sitting at the front: "Yes Rupert?"

Rupert (in a frightfully, frightfully, ever so plummy English accent): "Yes miss, that was Neil Armstrong, 1967, the first moon landing."

Teacher: "Very good Rupert. You may stay off Friday and Monday and come back into class on Tuesday."

Wee Hughie loses the plot altogether, tips his desk and throws his wee chair at the wall. He starts screaming, "Where the fuck did all these English bastards come from?"

The teacher spins back round from the blackboard and shouts, "Who said that?"

Wee Hughie grabs his coat and bag and heads for the door, "Bonnie Prince Charlie, Culloden, 1746. See ye on Tuesday, Miss."

The same teacher asks her class, "What was Churchill famous for?"

Wee Hughie shouts, "He was the last fucking white man in Britain to be called Winston."

The same teacher asked her students to use the word 'fascinate' in a sentence.

Shelley-Rose put up her hand and said, "My family went to my grandpa's farm, and we all saw his pet sheep. It was fascinating."

The teacher said, "That was good, but I wanted you to use the word 'fascinate', not 'fascinating'."

Sally raised her hand. She said, "My family went to see the Art Galleries and I was fascinated."

The teacher said, "Well, that was good Sally, but I wanted you to use the word 'fascinate', not 'fascinated'.

Wee Hughie raised his hand.

The teacher hesitated a bit because of previous encounters, but she finally decided there was no way he could damage the word 'fascinate', so she gave him the nod.

Wee Hughie said, "My auntie Gina has a sweater with ten buttons, but her tits are so big she can only fasten eight."

A five-year-old boy went to visit his Grandma one day. Playing with his toys in her bedroom while grandma was dusting, he looked up and said, "Grandma, how come you don't have a boyfriend now that Grandpa went to heaven?"

Grandma replied, "Dear, my TV is my boyfriend. I can sit in my bedroom and watch it all day long. The religious programmes make me feel good and

the comedies make me laugh. I'm happy with my TV as my boyfriend."

Grandma turned on the TV, and the reception was terrible. She started adjusting the knobs, trying to get the picture in focus. Frustrated, she started hitting the back of the TV, hoping to fix the problem.

The little boy heard the doorbell ring so he hurried to open the door and there stood Grandma's minister. The minister said, "Hello son, is your Grandma in?"

The little boy replied, "Aye, she's in the bedroom spanking her boyfriend."

A seven-year-old boy from Parkhead was at the centre of a court drama yesterday when he challenged a court ruling over who should have custody of him.

The boy has a history of being abused and beaten by his parents and the judge initially awarded custody to his aunt, in keeping with child custody law and regulations requiring that family unity be maintained to the degree possible.

The boy surprised the court when he proclaimed that his aunt abused and beat him more than his parents and he adamantly refused to live with her. When the judge then suggested that he live with his

grandparents, the boy cried out that they also beat him up. After considering the remainder of the immediate family and learning that domestic violence was apparently a way of life among them, the judge took the unprecedented step of allowing the boy to propose who should have custody of him.

After two breaks to check legal references and confer with child welfare officials, the judge granted temporary custody to Partick Thistle Football Club, whom the boy firmly believes are not capable of beating anyone.

2

PARKHEAD PUNTERS

A pal in Sydney sent me this. Someone in Motherwell copied it from a website and sent it to him. I've been unable to trace the author, undoubtedly an EastEnder, but if he or she cares to get in touch then the usual pint of lager or other drink of your choice will be available. He or she, with a linguistic talent like this, should be writing novels.

For those WestEnders suffering confusion, there are translations available if you Google the first line. None of them are as good as this.

The scene is Parkhead, Friday night.

Police officer. Yaw rite?
Driver. Maw rite.
Yeshoor?
Aye.
Zisyoors?
Zwitmine?
Ris caur.
Sibrurnlaws.

Wers heeren?

Raboozers.

Yebeen garglin'.

Jissa cupple.

Yur stoatin'.

Naw'mno'.

Ye urstoatin'.

Umnoe.

Geezyer licence.

Vno Goatwan.

Geroot racaur.

Whiffur?

Mapolis.

Ommigoad.

Geroot Ren.

Awrite, 'mcomin'.

Blawris up.

Mgonny Besik.

Noanme Yurno.

Mawrite Noo.

Getna Paddywagon.

Wer Wigaun?

Ra Jile.

Ohmigoad, rawife'll murder me.

Getna Wagon.

Aw, Neveragain. Ratsit furme.

A man is strolling past Parkhead Psychiatric Hospital in Salamander Street when he hears a loud chanting. "Thirteen, thirteen, thirteen!" goes the noise from the hospital.

The man's curiosity gets the better of him, and he searches for a hole in the security fence. It's not long before he finds a small crack, so he leans forward and peers in.

Instantly, someone jabs him in the eye. As he reels back in agony, the chanting continues. "Fourteen, fourteen, fourteen!"

A nurse walks into a room in Parkhead Psychiatric Hospital and sees a patient pretending he's driving a lorry, with his hands at 10 to 2. The nurse asks him, "Kenny, what are you doing?"

Kenny replies, "Can't talk right now, I'm driving to Devon." The nurse wishes him a good trip and leaves the room.

The next day the nurse enters Kenny's room just as he stops driving his imaginary truck and she asks, "Well Kenny, how was your trip?"

Kenny says, "I'm exhausted, I just got into Devon and I need some rest."

"That's great," replied the nurse, "I'm glad you had a safe trip."

The nurse leaves Kenny's room, and then goes

across the hall into another patient's room and finds Davy sitting on his bed masturbating vigorously.

Shocked, she shouts, "Davy, what are you doing?"

To which Davy replies, "Shhh, I'm shagging Kenny's wife while he's in Devon."

A man wearing a Celtic top was walking down the street in Parkhead and he met a small boy with the same strip. They got talking and the man asked his name.

The boy replied, "Six and seven-eighths."

The man asked him why his parents had given him such a strange name, and he replied, "They just picked it out of a hat."

Wee Hughie fae Parkhead, a man who loved completely atrocious puns, adored and admired his girl-friend, Lorraine, to whom he was engaged to be married. Wedding plans were well underway and he was looking forward to spending the rest of his life with Lorraine.

However, a beautiful young lady, called Clare-Leigh Maguire, came to work in his shop and they found that they got on together very well. As time went by, Wee Hughie realised that he was in love with Clare-Leigh and that the love was reciprocated. Being a gentleman, however, he decided that as he

had promised to marry Lorraine he would do so and steadily removed himself from his other relationship.

One day, he and Lorraine were walking down by Glasgow Green. As they walked, Lorraine slipped, fell into the Clyde and was swept away and drowned, as Mr Parsonage was busy elsewhere that day.

He stood on the bank for a few minutes feeling very sad before walking away singing happily, "I can see Clare-Leigh now Lorraine has gone."

A young couple from the Parkhead in the East End wanted to join the church and the minister told them, "We have a special requirement for new member couples. You must abstain from sex for one whole month." The couple agreed, but after two and a half weeks returned to the church.

When the minister ushered them into his office, the wife was crying and the husband was obviously very depressed. "You are back so soon. Is there a problem?" the pastor inquired.

"We are terribly ashamed to admit that we did not manage to abstain from sex for the required month," the young man replied sadly.

The minister asked him what happened.

"Well, the first week was difficult. . . . However, we managed to abstain through sheer willpower. The

second week was terrible, but with the use of prayer, we managed to abstain. However, the third week was unbearable. We tried cold showers, prayer, reading from the bible . . . anything to keep our minds off carnal thoughts. One afternoon my wife reached for a can of paint and dropped it. When she bent over to pick it up, I was overcome with lust and I just had my way with her right then and there. It was lustful, loud, passionate sex. It lasted for over an hour and when we were finished we were both drenched in sweat," admitted the man, shamefacedly.

The minister lowered his head and said sternly, "You understand this means you will not be welcome in our church."

"We know," said the young man, hanging his head. "We're not welcome at The Forge either."

Four men were being interviewed for a job.

The interviewer asked No. 1, "What is the fastest thing you know of?"

The first man replied, "A thought. It pops into your head, there's no forewarning that it's on the way; it's just there. A thought is the fastest thing I know of."

"That's very good," replied the interviewer.

"And now you," he asked No. 2.

"Hmmm, let me see . . . a blink!" said the second

man. "It comes and goes and you don't know it ever happened. A blink is the fastest thing I know of."

"Excellent!" said the interviewer. "The blink of an eye. That's a very popular cliché for speed."

He then turned to No. 3 who was contemplating his reply.

"Well, you step into my house and on the wall there is a light switch. When you flick that switch the light comes on in an instant. Turning on a light is the fastest thing I can think of."

The interviewer was very impressed with the third answer and thought he had found his man. "It's hard to beat the speed of light," he said.

Turning to the fourth man, an EastEnder, he posed the same question.

"After hearing the three previous answers, it's obvious to me the fastest thing known is diarrhoea," said the man.

"What?" said the interviewer, stunned by the response.

"Oh, I can explain," said the guy. "You see, the other day I wasn't feeling too well and ran for the bathroom. But, before I could think, blink, or turn on the light, I shit myself."

A man went down to Glasgow Green where a circus was in process. A sign read. "Don't Miss The

Amazing EastEnder". The man bought a ticket and sat down.

There, on centre stage, was a table with three walnuts on it. Standing next to it was an old guy from Tollcross.

Suddenly the old man lifted his kilt, whipped out his huge member and smashed all three walnuts with three mighty swings. The crowd erupted in applause as the elderly man was carried off on the shoulders of the crowd.

Ten years later the man saw the faded sign for the same circus and the same sign "Don't Miss The Amazing EastEnder". He couldn't believe the old guy was still alive much less still doing his act. He bought a ticket.

Again, the centre ring was illuminated. This time, however, instead of walnuts, three coconuts were placed on the table. The wee stooped kiltie stood before them, then suddenly lifted his kilt and smashed the coconuts with three swings of his amazing member.

The crowd went wild.

Flabbergasted, the man requested a meeting with him after the show.

"You're incredible!" he told the old guy. "But I have to know something. You're older now, why switch from walnuts to coconuts?"

"Well," said the performer, "my eyes are not what they used to be."

3

PUBS AND CLUBS

Two East End codgers are having a pint in the pub, and one says to the other, "I'm gettin' thoroughly sick and tired wi' oor dug."

"Whit fur?" says the other, "I thoat he wis a well behaved, intelligent dug?"

"Aye, usually he is," admits the first man, "but recently, he's taken tae chasin' anybuddy and everybuddy oan a bike."

"Oh," says the other, "so whit you gonny dae? Pit him in a dug's hame? Sell him? Gie him away?"

"Aw naw," says the first man, "Nothin' sae drastic. Ah'll just take his bike aff him."

There are several men sitting around in the changing room of an expensive West End private club (the only kind) after exercising. Suddenly a moby on one of the benches rings. A man picks it up, and the following conversation ensues.

"Hello?"

"Darling, it's me. Are you at the club?"

"Yes."

"Great! I am in town. I just saw a beautiful mink coat. It's absolutely gorgeous. Can I buy it?"

"What's the price?"

"Only £7,500."

"Well, OK, go ahead and get it, if you like it that much."

"Ahhh, and I also stopped by the Mercedes dealership and saw the 2009 models. I saw one I really liked. I spoke with the salesman, and he gave me a really good price, and since we need to exchange the BMW that we bought last year . . ."

"What price did he quote you?"

"Only £120,000."

"OK, but for that price I want it with all the options."

"Great! But before we hang up, there's something else."

"What?"

"It might look like a lot, but I was reconciling your bank account and I kind of stopped by the estate agent this morning and saw the house we looked at last year. It's still for sale. Remember? The one with the pool, 3 acre garden, the one in Strathbungo."

"How much are they asking?"

"Only £2,650,000 – cheap, cheap, cheap, darling, and I see that we have enough in the bank to cover it."

"Well, then go ahead and buy it, but just bid £2 mil, OK?"

"OK, sweetie. Thanks! I'll see you later. I love you!"

"Bye. I do too."

The man hangs up, holds up the phone and asks all those present,

"Okay . . . who owns this?"

A bloke walks into an East End pub and asks for 12 pints of Guinness. A mere hour later, he's drunk them all. He then asks the barman:

"Do you sell shorts?"

"Yes," he replies.

"Have you got any in a 38 waist, then? I've just shat these."

In the same pub three guys are drinking in the bar when a drunk comes in, staggers up to them, and points at the guy in the middle, shouting, "Your mum's the best sex in the East End."

Everyone expects a fight, but the guy ignores him, so the drunk wanders off and bellies up to the bar at the far end.

Ten minutes later, the drunk comes back, points at the same guy and says, "I just shagged your mum, and it was great."

Again the guy refuses to take the bait, and the drunk goes back to the far end of the bar.

Ten minutes later, he comes back and announces, "Your mum liked it!"

Finally the guy interrupts. "Go home, Dad, you're drunk!"

Horse walks in to the same bar and the barman asks, "What you havin?"

Horse replies, "Double whisky."

Barman asks, "Why the long face?"

Horse replies, "My mum just died."

A man and his dog walk into the same bar and the dog does a big dump in the middle of the floor. Another guy walks into the bar, skids on the shit and embarrassedly asks for a beer. A third man walks into the bar and does a huge skid straight on to his back, gets up cursing and walks to the bar. The second guy said to the third man, "I just did that." So he battered his lights in.

Same pub, a guy walks in and asks for a pint of lager and a packet of helicopter crisps.

"Sorry," said the barman, "we don't have any helicopter crisps, we only have plane."

4

AW THE NICE

Who said romance is dead? These are real ads from the lonely hearts columns of three East End local papers:

Grossly overweight Baillieston gambler, 42 years old and 23 stone, Gemini, seeks nimble sexpot, preferably South American, for tango sessions, candlelit dinners and humid nights of screaming passion. Must have own car and be willing to travel. Box 09/08

Parkhead man, 50, in desperate need of a ride. Anything considered. Box 06/03

Heavy drinker, 35, Shettleston area, seeks gorgeous sex addict interested in pints, fags, Celtic Football Club and starting fights in Sauchiehall Street at three in the morning. Box 73/82

Bitter, disillusioned, lately rejected by longtime fiancée seeks decent, honest, reliable woman, if such

a thing still exists in this cruel world of hatchet-faced bitches. Box /41

Ginger-haired Tollcross troublemaker, gets slit-eyed and shirty after a few scoops, seeks attractive, wealthy lady for bail purposes, maybe more. Box 84/87

Bad-tempered, foul-mouthed old bastard living in a damp cottage in the arse end of Baillieston seeks attractive 21-year-old blonde lady with big chest. Box 40/27

Devil worshipper, Parkhead area, seeks like-minded lady for wining and dining, good conversation, dancing, romantic walks and slaughtering dogs in the Eastern Necropolis at midnight under the flinty light of a pale moon. Box 52/07

Attractive East End brunette, now in Maryhill area, winner of Miss Wrangler competition at Frampton's Nightclub, Maryhill, in September 1978, seeks nostalgic man who's not afraid to cry, for long nights spent comfort drinking and listening to old Abba records. Please, Please! Box 30/41

Garngad man, 27, medium build, brown hair, blue eyes, seeks alibi for the night of February 27 between 8pm and 11.30pm

Artistic Shettleston woman, 53, petite, loves rainy walks on the beach, writing poetry, unusual seashells and interesting brown rice dishes, seeks mystic dreamer for companionship, back rubs and more as we bounce along like little tumbling clouds on life's beautiful crazy journey. Strong stomach essential. Box 12/32

Chartered accountant, 42, Dennistoun, seeks female for marriage. Duties will include cooking, light cleaning and accompanying me to office social functions. References required. No timewasters. Box 3/45

5

CRETINS AND CRIMS

East End Paddy wins the lottery. Camelot says, "We're running low on funds. Can we give you £3 million this week and £3 million next week?"

Paddy says, "If you're gonny fuck me aboot, just gies ma pound back".

Two West End businessmen in Great Western Road were sitting down for a break in their soon-to-be-new shop. As yet, the store wasn't ready, with only a few shelves set up.

One said to the other, "I bet you that any minute now some idiot is going to walk by, put his face to the window, and ask what we're selling."

No sooner were the words out of his mouth when, sure enough, a curious EastEnder, on a visit to see what civilization was like, walked to the window, had a peek, and asked, "What are you selling here?"

One of the men replied sarcastically, "We're selling arseholes."

Without skipping a beat, the EastEnder said, "You're doing well. Only two left."

A West End blonde gets a job as a teacher in the East End. She notices a boy in the field standing alone, while all the other kids are running around. She takes pity on him and decides to speak to him.

"You ok?" she says.

"Aye," he says.

"You can go and play with the other children you know," she says.

"It's best I stay here," he says.

"Why?" says the blonde.

The boy says, "Because I'm the fucking goalie."

EastEnders Mick and Paddy had promised their uncle Seamus, who had been a seafaring gent all his life, to bury him at sea when he died. Of course, in due time, he did pass away and the boys kept their promise. They set off with Uncle Seamus all stitched up in a Celtic flag bag and loaded him on to a hired rowing boat. After a while Mick says, "Do you think this is far enough out, Paddy?"

Without a word Paddy slips over the side only to find himself standing in water up to his knees. "This will never do, Mick. Let's row a bit more."

After a bit more rowing Paddy slips over the side again but the water is only up to his belly, so they row on.

Again Mick asks Paddy, "Do you think this is far enough out Paddy?"

Once again Paddy slips over the side and almost immediately says, "No, this will never do." The water was only up to his chest.

So on they row and row and row and finally Paddy slips over the side and disappears. Quite a bit of time goes by and poor Mick is really getting himself into a state when suddenly Paddy breaks the surface gasping for breath. "Well is it deep enough yet, Paddy?"

"Aye it is, hand me the shovel."

EastEnder Paddy met Mick in the street and said, "Paddy, could you draw your bedroom curtains before making love to your wife in future?"

"Why?" Paddy asked.

"Because," said Mick, "the whole street was laughing when they saw you making love yesterday."

Mick said, "Silly bastards, the laugh's on them. I wasn't at home yesterday."

A little boy from St Jude's, who will go far in the world if he lives, was praying as hard as he could.

"Jesus," he prayed, "I really want a pony." Jumping

up and dashing to the window, he saw that the street was empty.

"Jesus," he prayed again, "I really NEED a pony."

Still, no answer to his prayers.

Suddenly the laddie stood up, ran into his parent's bedroom, and grabbed the statuette of the Virgin Mary off the mantelpiece.

He wrapped it up in ten layers of paper, using three rolls of tape and a whole ball of string, then stuffed it inside a box at the very bottom of his wardrobe.

"Okay, Jesus," he said, getting down onto his knees again, "If you ever want to see your mother again."

An Anglican vicar went into that wee barber shop in the Barras, had his hair cut, thanked the barber, and asked how much he owed him. The barber said, "Reverend, you're a man of the cloth, I couldn't charge you. It's on the house."

"That's frightfully decent of you, old chap," said the vicar, and left. The next day, on the doorstep of the barber shop were twelve bibles.

A few days later, a priest went in for a shave, and when the time came to pay the barber said, "Father, you're a man of the cloth, I couldn't charge you. It's on the house."

"That's very kind. Bless you," said the priest, and

left. The next day, on the doorstep were twelve bottles of wine.

The following week a Church of Scotland minister came in, had his hair cut, went to pay and the barber said, "Sir, you're a man of the cloth, I couldn't charge you. It's on the house."

"Thanks," said the minister. "Cheerio."

And the next day, on the doorstep of the barber shop were twelve Church of Scotland ministers.

In ancient Easterhoose (AD 1965), Wise Wullie was widely lauded for his wisdom. One day an acquaintance ran up to him excitedly and said, "Wise Wullie, do you know what I just heard about one of your students called Shagger McGraw?"

"Wait a moment," Wise Wullie replied. "Before you tell me I'd like you to pass a little test. It's called the Triple Filter Test."

"Triple filter?"

"That's right," Wise Wullie continued. "Before you talk to me about my student, let's take a moment to filter what you're going to say. The first Filter is Truth. Have you made absolutely sure that what you are about to tell me is true?"

"No," the man said, "actually I just heard about it and . . ."

"All right," said Wise Wullie. "So you don't really know if it's true or not. Now let's try the second filter, the Filter of Goodness. Is what you are about to tell me about my student something good?"

"No, on the contrary . . ."

"So," Wise Wullie continued, "you want to tell me something bad about him, even though you're not certain it's true?" The man shrugged, a little embarrassed.

Wise Wullie continued. "You may still pass the test though, because there is a third filter – the Filter of Usefulness. Is what you want to tell me about my student going to be useful to me?"

"No, not really . . ."

"Well," concluded Wise Wullie, "if what you want to tell me is neither True, nor Good, nor even Useful, why tell it to me at all?" The man was defeated and ashamed.

This is the reason Wise Wullie was a great philosopher and held in such high esteem. It also explains why he never found out that Shagger McGraw was shagging Wise Wullie's wife.

A big time West End lawyer is driving through the East End and comes to a stop sign. He slows down, sees nothing is coming, so moves through.

He's immediately flagged down by one of Glasgow's finest.

The polis: "Right pal, you just drove through a stop sign, am booking ye."

Lawyer: "This is ridiculous, I slowed right down and the junction was free, what's the problem?"

The polis: "It says stop, no slow doon. Yer nicked."

Lawyer: " Look, this is silly. A technicality. Tell you what – if you can give me a good example between slowing or stopping, I won't contest the case."

The Polis: "Get oot the car." Polis draws his baton and proceeds to batter the lawyer.

Lawyer, screaming in pain, shouts: "Stop! Stop!"

The polis: "Ok, but dae ye want me tae stop or just slow doon a bit?"

There was a Russian wrestler called Ivan the Terrible. Everyone was scared of him because he had two famous holds – the Half-Nelson and the Full-Nelson. The Half-Nelson broke your back and the Full-Nelson killed you. So there was a huge trail of dead bodies all over Russia until nobody would fight him any more.

So, he joined the circus. "A thousand pounds to any man who can last one round with the dreaded Ivan the Terrible," said the ringmaster.

All the crowd shrank into their seats muttering, "I'm no fightin' that!"

The circus goes all across Europe, up into France and then one day the circus came to Glasgow Green.

"A thousand pounds to any man who . . ."

"I'll dae it!!" said a wee skinny man, about three stone four with big heavy boots and glasses.

"Do you know what you are doing, sir?" asked the ringmaster.

"Aye."

So he climbs into the ring and from behind the curtain someone hooks a shepherd's crook around Ivan's neck and shoves him out.

"GRRRRRRR," said Ivan, easily six foot eight, all hair and teeth.

The crowd start to chant, "Gaun, Shuggy, intae him, intae him."

"Relax boys, it's a doddle. Here we go," said the skinny one.

The two of them meet in the centre of the ring and clash together.

They scrum on the floor and then Ivan flips a skinny arm over.

"Aw naw!" says the crowd, "The HALF-NEL-SON!!"

Ivan wraps another arm over.

"Aw naw!" booms the crowd, "THE FULL-NEL-SON!!"

They fall to the floor again amid cries of agony and sweaty grunting.

Then BANG! Ivan comes spinning off, hits the wall and slides down unconscious.

The crowd is hysterical. "Gaun, Shuggy, we are the champions!"

The skinny bloke is being interviewed by the BBC. "Tell me Mr Shugg, how did it feel to win a thousand pounds?"

"No too bad, thanks Tam."

"And just how did you achieve this amazing defeat?"

"Och, it wis a doddle, man. There we wis, rolling aboot oan the flerr, when I felt the life draining right oot me. Then I sees it, right there in front of me, a huge willy! I thinks to masel, 'now haud on a wee minute'. But then I thought 'what the hell' and sank ma teeth right intae it. And ye know something? It's amazing the super-strength ye get when ye bite yer ain willy!"

While walking through Kelvingrove Park a man came upon another man hugging a tree with his ear firmly against it. Seeing this he enquired, "Just out of curiosity, what are you doing?"

"I'm listening to the music of the tree," the other man replied.

"You're kiddin' me."

"No, would you like to give it a try?"

Understandably curious, the man says, "Well, OK . . ." So he wrapped his arms around the tree and pressed his ear up against it. With this, the other man whacks a pair of handcuffs on his wrists, took his wallet, phone, and car keys, then stripped him naked and left.

Two hours later another nature lover strolled by, saw this guy handcuffed to the tree stark naked, and asked, "What happened to you?" He told the guy the whole terrible story about how he got there. When he finished telling his story, the other guy shook his head in sympathy, walked around behind him, kissed him gently behind the ear and said, "This just isn't going to be your day, pretty one."

A WestEnder was out at Shawfield, all but losing his shirt. Then Peter noticed a priest who stepped out onto the track and blessed the forehead of one of the dogs lining up for the fourth race. Lo and behold, that dog, a very long shot, won the race. Before the next race, as the dogs began lining up, Peter watched with interest the old priest step onto the track. Sure enough, as the fifth race dogs came

to the start the priest made a blessing on the fore-head of one of the dogs.

Peter made a beeline for a bookie and placed a small bet on the dog. Again, even though it was another long shot, the dog the priest had blessed won the race. Peter collected his winnings, and anxiously waited to see which dog the priest would bless for the sixth race. The priest again blessed a dog.

Peter bet a lot on it, and it won. Peter was elated. As the races continued the priest kept blessing long shot dogs, and each one ended up coming in first. By and by, Peter was pulling in some serious money. By the last race, he knew his wildest dreams were going to come true. He made a quick dash to the Cashline, withdrew all his savings, and awaited the priest's blessing that would tell him which dog to bet on.

True to his pattern, the priest stepped onto the track for the last race and blessed the forehead of an old greyhound that was the longest shot of the day. Peter also observed the priest blessing the eyes, ears, and feet of the old dog.

Peter knew he had a winner and bet every penny he owned on the old dog. He then watched dumb-founded as the dog came in dead last and then died. Peter, in a state of shock, made his way down to the track area where the priest was.

Confronting the old priest he demanded, "Father!

What happened? All day long you blessed dogs and they all won. Then in the last race, the dog you blessed lost by a mile. Now, thanks to you I've lost every penny of my savings. All of it."

The priest nodded wisely and with sympathy. "Son," he said, "that's the problem with you Proddies, you can't tell the difference between a simple blessing and the last rites."

An 80-year-old EastEnder goes to the doctor for a check-up. The doctor is amazed at what good shape the guy is in and asks, "How do you stay in such great physical condition?"

"I am a golfer," says the old guy. "I'm up well before daylight and out golfing up and down the fairways. Have a wee nip of whisky, and all is well."

"Well," says the doctor, "I'm sure that helps, but there's got to be more to it. How old was your Dad when he died?"

"Who said my Dad's dead?"

The doctor is amazed, "You mean you're 80 years old and your Dad's still alive. How old is he?"

"He's 100 years old," says the man. "In fact he golfed with me this morning, and then we went to the pub for a whisky and for a walk, and that's why he's still alive. He's a Highlander and he's a golfer, too."

"Well," the doctor says, "that's great, but I'm sure there's more to it than that. How about your Dad's Dad? How old was he when he died?"

"Who said my grandpa's dead?"

Stunned, the doctor asks, "You mean you're 80 years old and your grandfather's still living! Incredible, how old is he?"

"He's 118 years old," says the guy.

The doctor is getting frustrated at this point, "So, I suppose he went golfing with you this morning, too?"

"No. Grandpa couldn't go this morning because he's getting married today."

At this point the doctor is close to losing it. "Getting married! Why would a 118-year-old guy want to get married?"

"Who said he wanted to?"

Germ-conscious West End John went to visit his 90-year-old grandfather in a very secluded, rural area of Sutherland. After spending a great evening chatting the night away, and a good night's sleep, John's grandfather prepared a breakfast of bacon, eggs and toast.

However, John noticed a film like substance on his plate, and questioned his grandfather asking, "Are these plates clean?"

His grandfather replied, "They're as clean as cold

water can get them. Just you go ahead and finish your meal, Sonny Jim."

For lunch the old man made mince. Again, John was concerned about the plates as his appeared to have tiny specks around the edge that looked like dried egg and he asked, "Are you sure these plates are clean?"

Without looking up, the old man said, "I told you before, lad, those dishes are as clean as cold water can get them. Now don't you fret, I don't want to hear another word about it."

Later that afternoon, John was on his way to a nearby town and as he was leaving, his grandfather's dog started to growl, and wouldn't let him pass.

John yelled and said, "Grandfather, your dog won't let me get to my car."

Without diverting his attention from assembling his fishing rod, the old man shouted, "COLDWA-TER!"

What would you call it when a WestEnder has one arm shorter than the other?

A speech impediment.

West End /East End translations
West End. Maxwell, you are being terribly annoy-ing, please leave.

East End. Pick a windae, cuntface.

Three East End guys named Steve, Bruce and Kevin were working on a high rise building. Steve falls off and is killed instantly.

As the ambulance takes the body away, Bruce says, "Someone should go and tell his wife."

Kevin says, "OK, I'm pretty good at that sensitive stuff, I'll do it."

Two hours later, he comes back carrying a case of Tennent's Lager.

Bruce says, "Where did you get that, Kev?"

"Steve's wife gave it to me," Bruce replies.

"That's unbelievable, you told the woman her husband was dead and she gave you the beer?"

"Well not exactly," Kevin said. "When she answered the door, I said to her. 'You must be Steve's widow'. She said, 'No, I'm not a widow.' And I said, 'I'll bet you a case of Tennents you are'."

6

WISE WOMEN

Morag was driving home to Cranhill from one of her business trips when she saw an elderly nun walking on the side of the road just outside Stirling. As the trip was a long and quiet one, she stopped the car and asked the nun if she would like a lift. With a silent nod of thanks, the woman got into the car.

Resuming the journey, Morag tried in vain to make a bit of small talk with the elderly lady. The old woman just sat silently, looking intently at everything she saw, studying every little detail, until she noticed a brown bag on the seat next to Morag.

"What's in the bag?" asked the old woman.

Morag looked down at the brown bag and said, "It's a bottle of wine. I got it for my husband."

The nun was silent for another moment or two, then speaking with the quiet wisdom of an elder, she said, "Good swap."

It was Mount Vernon and the polis was making his evening rounds. As he was checking a second hand car sales lot, he came upon two wee old biddies sit-

ting in a car. He stopped and asked them why they were sitting there in the car.

Were they trying to steal it? "No, no, son, we bought it."

"Then why don't you drive it away?"

"We canny drive."

"Then why did you buy it?"

"We were told that if we bought a used car here we'd get fucked. So we're just waiting."

An East End man was having an affair with his secretary. One day they went to her place and made love all afternoon. Exhausted, they fell asleep and woke up at 8pm.

The man hurriedly dressed and told his lover to take his shoes outside and rub them in the grass and dirt. He put on his shoes and drove home.

"Where have you been?" his wife demanded.

"I can't lie to you," he replied. "I'm having an affair with my secretary. We had sex all afternoon."

"You lying bastard! You've been playing golf!"

An East End woman came home just in time to find her husband in bed with another woman. With superhuman strength borne out of fury, she dragged her husband down the stairs to the garage and put his wedding tackle in the vice. She then secured it

tightly and removed the handle. Next she picked up a hacksaw. The husband terrified, screamed, "Stop! Stop! You're not going to . . . to . . . cut it off are you?"

The wife, with a glint of revenge in her eye, said, "No. You are. I'm going to set the garage on fire."

There's a new study just released by the Psychiatric Association about East End women and how they feel about their arses. The results are pretty interesting.

1. 5% of women surveyed feel their arse is too big.

2. 10% of women surveyed feel their arse is too small.

3. The remaining 85% say they don't care; they love him, he's a good man and they would have married him anyway.

Dear Lord,

   I pray for Wisdom to understand my man;
   Love to forgive him;
   And Patience for his moods;
   Because Lord, if I pray for Strength,
   I'll beat the bastard to death.

A married couple in their early 60s were celebrating their 35th wedding anniversary in a quiet, romantic little restaurant.

Suddenly, a tiny beautiful fairy appeared on their table saying, "For being such an exemplary married couple and for being loving to each other for all this time, I will grant you each a wish."

"Oh, I want to travel around the world with my darling husband," said the woman.

The fairy waved her magic wand and poof (it's a West End fairy) two tickets for a cruise appeared in her hands.

The husband thought for a moment. "Well, this is all very romantic, but an opportunity like this will never come again. I'm sorry my love, but my wish is to have a wife 30 years younger than me."

The wife and the fairy were deeply disappointed, but a wish is a wish. So the fairy waved her magic wand and poof!

The husband became 92 years old.

The moral of this story.

Men who are ungrateful bastards should remember, fairies are female.

Except of course in the West End.

Four women, all of whom had sons, attended a party. Three were from Hillhead, one from Parkhead. As is

usually the case with mothers, talk turned to their children. The first woman said, "My son is my pride and joy. He started working at a successful company at the bottom of the barrel. He studied Economics and Business Administration and soon began to climb the business ladder and now he's the MD of the company. He became so rich that he gave his best friend a Mercedes for his birthday."

The second woman said, "My son is also my pride and joy. He started working for a big airline, then went to flight school to become a pilot. Eventually he became a partner in the company, where he owns the majority of its assets. He's so rich that he gave his best friend a brand new jet for his birthday."

The third woman said, "My son is also my pride and joy. He studied in the best universities and became an engineer. Then he started his own construction company and is now a millionaire. He also gave away something very nice and expensive to his best friend for his birthday. A nice big house."

It was the fourth woman's turn, the EastEnder. "My son is gay and makes a living dancing as a stripper at a nightclub."

Her three new friends said, "What a shame. You must be terribly disappointed."

The mother smiled. "No, he is my pride and joy. He's my son and I love him. And he hasn't done too

badly either. His birthday was two weeks ago, and he received a nice big house, a brand new jet and a top of the line Mercedes from his three boyfriends."

An East End man was sick and tired of going to work every day while his wife stayed at home. He wanted her to see what he went through so he prayed.

"Dear Lord. I go to work every day and put in 8 hours while my wife stays at home. I want her to know what I go through, so please allow her body to switch with mine for a day. Amen."

God, in his infinite wisdom, granted the man's wish. The next morning, sure enough, the man awoke as a woman.

He arose,
cooked breakfast for his partner,
wakened the kids,
set out their school clothes,
fed them breakfast,
packed their lunches,
drove them to school,
came home and
picked up the dry cleaning,
took it to the cleaners and
stopped at the bank,

went shopping,
then drove home to put away the groceries,
paid the bills and
balanced the books.
He cleaned the cat's litter box and bathed the dog.

Then it was 1pm
and he hurried to make the beds,
do the laundry,
vacuum,
dust, and
sweep and
mop the kitchen floor.
Ran to the school to pick up the kids and
got into an argument with them on the way home.
Set out milk and Coco Pops and
got the kids organised to do their homework,
then set up the ironing board and
watched TV while he did the ironing.

At 4.30
he began peeling potatoes and
washing vegetables for salad,
got out the pork chops and
fresh green beans for tea.
After tea, he cleaned the kitchen,
Washed the dishes,

folded the laundry,
bathed the kids, and
put them to bed.

At 9pm
he was exhausted and,
though his daily chores weren't finished,
he went to bed where he was expected to make love,
which he managed to get through without complaint.

The next morning, he awoke and immediately knelt by the bed and said, "Lord, I don't know what I was thinking. I was so wrong to envy my wife's being able to stay home all day. Please, please, let us swop back."

The Lord, in his infinite wisdom, replied, "My son, I feel you have learned your lesson and I will be happy to change things back to the way they were. You'll have to wait a wee while, though. You got pregnant last night."

A West End wife came home early and found her husband in their bedroom making love to a very attractive young woman. The wife was very upset. "You are a disrespectful pig," she cried. "How dare

you do this to me? A faithful wife, the mother of your children! I'm leaving you. I want a divorce."

And he replied, "Hang on just a minute, luv, so at least I can tell you what happened."

"Fine, go ahead," she sobbed, "but they'll be the last words you say to me!"

And he began, "I was getting into the car in Parkhead to drive home and this young woman here asked me for a lift. She looked so down and out and defenceless that I took pity on her and let her into the car. I noticed that she was very thin, not well dressed and very dirty. She told me that she hadn't eaten for three days. So, in my compassion, I brought her home and warmed up the mince I made for you last night which you wouldn't eat because you're afraid you'll put on weight. The poor thing devoured it in moments.

"Since she needed a good clean up I suggested a shower and while she was doing that I noticed her clothes were dirty and full of holes, so I threw them away. Then, as she needed clothes, I gave her the designer jeans that you have had for a few years, but don't wear because you say they are too tight.

"I also gave her the underwear that was your anniversary present, which you don't wear because I don't have good taste. I also found the sexy blouse

my sister gave you for Christmas that you don't wear just to annoy her and I also donated those boots you bought at the expensive boutique and don't wear because someone at work has a pair like them."

He took a quick breath and continued, "She was so grateful for my understanding and help and as I walked her to the door she turned to me with tears in her eyes and said, "Please, do you have anything else that your wife doesn't use?"

A young mixed-marriage (he was from the West, she was from the East) couple left the church and arrived at the hotel where they were spending the first night of their honeymoon. They opened the champagne and began undressing. When the bride-groom removed his socks, his new wife asked, "Ewww, what's wrong with your feet? Your toes look all mangled and terrible. Why are your feet so ugly?"

"I had tolio as a child," he answered.

"You mean polio?" she asked.

"No, tolio. The disease only affected my toes."

The bride was satisfied with this explanation, and they continued undressing. When the groom took off his trousers, his bride once again wrinkled up her nose.

"What's wrong with your knees?" she asked. "They're all lumpy and deformed."

"As a child, I also had kneasles," he explained.

"You mean measles?" she asked.

"No, kneasles. It was a strange illness that only affected my knees."

The new bride had to be satisfied with this answer. As the undressing continued, her husband at last removed his underwear. She looked down at his willie.

"Don't tell me," she said. "Let me guess. Smallcox?"

A West End woman comes home and tells her husband, "Remember those headaches I've been having all these years? Well, they're gone."

"No more headaches?" the husband asks. "What happened?"

His wife replies, "Margie referred me to a hypnotist. He told me to stand in front of a mirror, stare at myself and repeat:

"I do not have a headache.

"I do not have a headache.

"I do not have a headache.

"It worked. The headaches are all gone."

His wife then says, "You know, you haven't been exactly the bees' knees in the bedroom these last few years. Why don't you go see the hypnotist and see if he can do anything for that?"

The husband agrees to try it.

Following his appointment, the husband comes home, rips off his clothes, picks up his wife and carries her into the bedroom. He puts her on the bed and says, "Don't move, I'll be right back."

He goes into the bathroom and comes back a few minutes later and jumps into bed and makes passionate love to his wife like never before.

His wife says, "Jesus, Tom, that was wonderful!"

The husband says, "Don't move! I'll be right back."

He goes back into the bathroom, comes back and round two is even better than the first time. The wife sits up and her head is spinning.

Her husband again says, "Don't move, I'll be right back."

With that, he goes back into the bathroom.

This time, his wife quietly follows him and there, in the bathroom, she sees him standing at the mirror and saying,

"She's not my wife.

"She's not my wife.

"She's not my wife."

7

OLDIES AND GOLDIES

A pregnant teenage girl phones her dad at midnight and says, "Can you come and get me? I think ma water has broken."

"Okay," says her dad. "Where are you ringing frae?"

"Frae ma knickers tae ma feet."

A Glasgow woman goes to the dentist and settles down in the chair.

"Comfy?" asks the dentist.

"Govan," she replies.

A guy walks into an antiques shop and says, "How much for the set of antlers?"

"Two hundred quid," says the bloke behind the counter.

"That's affa dear," says the guy.

Did you hear about the fella who liked eating bricks and cement?

He's awa' noo.

After announcing he's getting married, a boy tells his pal he'll be wearing the kilt.

"And what's the tartan?" asks his mate.

"Oh, she'll be wearing a white dress."

Ten cows in a field. Which one is closest to Iraq ?
Coo eight.

An EastEnder in London is having trouble phoning his sister from a telephone box, so he calls the operator who asks, "Is there money in the box?"

"Naw, it's just me," he replies.

While getting ready to go out, a wee wifie asks her husband, "Do you think I'm getting a wee bit pigeon-chested?"

And he says, "Aye, but that's why I love you like a doo."

What was the name of the first Scottish cowboy?
Hawkeye The Noo.

What do you call a pigeon that goes to Aviemore for its holidays?
A skean dhu.

How many Spanish guys does it take to change a lightbulb?

Just the Juan.

What's the difference between The Rolling Stones and an Aberdeen shepherd?

The Rolling Stones say, "Hey you, get off of my cloud."

And an Aberdeen shepherd says, "Hey McLeod, get off of ma ewe."

Did you hear about the BBC Scotland series that features the queue for the toilets at Waverley Station? It's called The Aw' Needin' Line.

While being interviewed for a job as a bus driver, a guy is asked, "What would you do if you had a rowdy passenger?"

"I'd put him off at the next stop," he says.

"Good. And what would you do if you couldn't get the fare?"

"I'd take the first two weeks in August."

A man, steaming and skint, is walking down Argyle Street when he spots a guy tinkering with the engine of his car. "What's up Jimmy?" he asks.

"Piston broke," he replies.

"Aye, same as masel."

I fancied a game of darts with my mate. He said, "Nearest the bull goes first."

He went "Baah" and I went "Moo". He said, "You're closest."

I was driving up the motorway and my boss phoned me and he told me I'd been promoted. I was so shocked I swerved the car. He phoned me again to say I'd been promoted even higher and I swerved again. He then made me managing director and I went right off into a tree. The police came and asked me what had happened. I said, "I careered off the road."

A flat-chested young EastEnder wanted to enlarge her breasts and went to a popular plastic surgeon known for 'no scars'. To her shock, Dr McDonald advised her, "Every day, after your shower, rub your chest and say, "Scooby doobie dooby, I want bigger boobies." He guaranteed success and, thinking she had nothing to lose, she did what he told her to do faithfully for several months.

To her utter amazement she grew terrific D-cup boobs. One morning, she was running late, got on the bus, and in a panic realized she had forgotten her morning ritual.

Frightened she might lose her lovely breasts if she didn't recite the little rhyme, she stood right there in the middle aisle of the bus, closed her eyes and said quietly, "Scooby doobie dooby, I want bigger boobies."

She apparently didn't say it quietly enough, though, since a guy sitting nearby looked at her and asked, "Are you a patient of Dr McDonald?"

"Yes, I am," she said, a bit embarrassed. "How did you know?"

He winked and whispered quietly, "Hickory dickory dock."

8

MEDICAL MISHAPS

Things you don't want to hear on the operating table, whether it be Gartnavel or The Royal.

1. Better save that. We'll need it for the post mortem.

2. Accept this sacrifice, O Great Lord of Darkness.

3. Lassie! Lassie! Come back with that. Bad dog!

4. Wait a minute, if this is his spleen, then what's that?

5. Hand me that ehm, that ehm, that thingy there.

6. Oh no. Where's my Rolex?

7. Oops! Has anyone ever survived from 500ml of this stuff before?

8. There go the lights again!

9. You know, there's good money in kidneys and this guy's got two of them.

10. Everybody stand back. I've lost my contact lens.

11. Could you stop that thing from beating; it's fucking up my concentration.

12. What's this doing here?

13. I hate it when they're missing stuff in here.

14. That's cool. Now can you make his leg twitch by pressing that one?

15. Well folks, this will be an experiment for all of us.

16. Sterile? The floor's clean, right?

17. What do you mean he wasn't in for a sex change?!

18. OK, now take a picture from this angle. This is truly a freak of nature.

19. This patient has already had some kids, am I correct?

20. Nurse, did this patient sign an organ donation card?

21. Don't worry. I think it's sharp enough.

22. What do you mean, "I want a divorce?"

23. Fire! Fire! Everyone get out!

24. Shit. Page 47 of the manual is missing.

A Hillhead guy fell asleep on the beach at Millport for several hours during the only sunny day there this year and got horrible sunburn, specifically on his upper legs. He was sent to the Western Infirmary and was promptly admitted and diagnosed with second degree burns. With his skin already starting to blister and the severe pain he was in, the young doctor ordered continuous intravenous feeding with saline, electrolytes, a sedative and a viagra pill every four hours. The nurse, who was rather astounded, asked, "What good will the viagra do him, doctor?"

The doctor replied, "It won't do anything for his condition but it will keep the sheets off his legs."

A wee old man shuffled slowly into a café in Alexandra Parade, and pulled himself slowly, painful-

ly, up on to a stool. After catching his breath he ordered a banana split. The waitress asked kindly. "Crushed nuts?"

"Naw," he replied, "arthritis."

9

SECTARIANISM? SURELY NOT IN THIS DAY AND AGE

A WestEnder wearing a Rangers top crashes his motor and awakens from the surgery to find himself in the care of nuns. As he was recovering, a nun asked him questions regarding how he was going to pay for his treatment.

She asked if he had private health insurance.

He replied in a raspy voice, "No private health insurance."

The nun asked if he had any money in the bank.

He replied, "No money in the bank."

The nun asked, "Do you have a relative who could help you?"

He said, "I only have a spinster sister who is a nun."

The nun became agitated and announced loudly, "Nuns are not spinsters! Nuns are married to God."

The guy said, "Send the bill to my brother-in-law."

Father Murphy is fed up with the Protestant and

Catholic nonsense after the Celtic vs Rangers game so goes down the Orange Hall and says, "Let's get together and have a quiz night." The Orange Hall agreed and sent a team round.

Father Murphy says, "Let's get started, boys. First question is: who scored the first goal for Celtic in the European Cup Final in Lisbon?"

Pat: beep . . . "That was Tommy Gemmell."

Father Murphy: "Correct".

Billy: "Here, ah hope they are not all going to be like that."

Father Murphy: "No, my child they are not. Next question: who was the first Scottish team to do nine in a row?"

Pat: beep . . . "That was Celtic."

Father Murphy: "Correct."

Billy: "Here, ah thought you said they wurnae aw like that."

Father Murphy: "Of course they're not. Next question: who scored for Rangers in the League cup final?"

Billy: beep . . . "Whit league cup final was that?"

Father Murphy: "Oh Hampden in the sun, Celtic seven and the Rangers one".

A Scottish golfer playing in Ireland hooked his drive into the woods. Looking for his ball, he found a

little leprechaun flat on his back, a big bump on his head and the golfer's ball beside him.

Horrified, the golfer got his water bottle from the cart and poured it over the wee guy, reviving him.

"Arrgh! What happened?" the leprechaun asked.

"I'm afraid I hit you with my golf ball," the golfer says.

"Oh, I see. Well, ye got me fair and square. Ye get three wishes, so what do you want?"

"Thank God, you're all right!" the golfer answers in relief. "I don't want anything, I'm just glad you're OK, and I apologise."

And the golfer walks off. "What a nice guy," the leprechaun says to himself. "I have to do something for him. I'll give him the three things I would want – a great golf style, all the money he ever needs, and a fantastic sex life."

A year goes by (as it does in stories like this) and the Scottish golfer is back. On the same hole, he again hits a bad drive into the woods and the leprechaun is there waiting for him.

"Twas me that made ye hit the ball here," the little guy says. "I just want to ask ye, how's yer game?"

"My game is fantastic," the golfer answers. "I'm an internationally famous amateur golfer now." He adds, "By the way, it's good to see that you're all right."

"Oh, I'm fine now, thank ye. I did that for yer golf game, you know. And tell me, how's yer money situation?"

"Why, it's just wonderful!" the golfer states. "When I need cash, I just reach into my pocket and pull out money I didn't even know was there."

"I did that fer ye also. And tell me, how's yer sex life?" The golfer blushes, turns his head away in embarrassment, and says shyly, "It's OK."

"Ah c'mon now," urged the Leprechaun, "I'm wanting to know if I did a good job. How many times a week?"

Blushing even more, the golfer looks around then whispers, "Once, sometimes twice a week."

"What?" responds the Leprechaun in shock. "That's all? Only once or twice a week?"

"Well," says the golfer, "that's not bad for a Catholic priest in an East End parish."

10

BLACKHILL BORN AND BRED

There has been a lot said about Blackhill, most of it lies, some of it by me, not much of it pleasant, but here's a true story with pleasant bits.

Back in the dim and distant, 1990, if memory serves, Libby McArthur, currently playing Gina Rossi in River City, was the community arts officer for Blackhill and put on a play what she wrote. It was titled 'Blackhill Born and Bred' and had a great song with that title, written by Libby. For reasons I can't remember, but probably because she is a chum, despite her coming from Castlemilk, I went to see the play.

In it there was a young lad called Kevin, and he was terrific. Fast forward a week or two and I get a call from another chum, Kenny Ireland, currently playing that mad Scottish expat in Benidorm, but then intent on directing 'The Bevellers', Roddy McMillan's play about the last hurrah of the Glasgow glass houses, at The Royal Lyceum in Edinburgh. Do I know a youngster who might be interested in playing the new-start apprentice? I

think of Kevin, call Libby, he goes to see Kenny and gets the gig. Well done, good deed done for the year, I think, chums and Kevin happy, win/win situation, and forget it.

Then I get a call from Libby. Blackhill is marshalling behind Kevin and a bus has been organized for the first night. Do I want to be on it? I do indeedy, I think, and whistle myself along to Blackhill for one of the most bizarre theatrical experiences of my life.

Most of the people on the bus, and they were smashing folk, had never been in a theatre before. And this was, excuse the capitals, THE ROYAL LYCEUM. In Edinburgh, bastion of the middle classes. Certain behavior was required of the lower classes from Blackhill. Didn't happen.

The Lyceum, God love them, had given the Blackhill people some thought, did not want all of us sitting together, and had given us wee sets of two or three seats all over the theatre. Didn't happen. No overt threats were made, but somehow we became the first two rows of the balcony.

Did I mention the kerry-oots? I had never before then, and certainly not since, drunk Diamond White cider mixed with Buckfast in a bus on my way to a play, or indeed on my way to anywhere, and I have never since taken a kerry-oot into a play. We

were required to turn said kerry-oots over to the authorities. Didn't happen. Much bottle clinking, much hilarity, play starts.

Good play, good actors, good behavior from us, no heckling, nothing inappropriate. Then Kevin made his entrance. Pandefuckingmonium, as it was later described to me by one of our group. Well-known and respected actors used to get a round of applause, a smattering of appreciation on an entrance, but not the first two rows of the balcony on its collective feet bellowing. "Kevin! Kevin!" for a first professional appearance.

Kevin, to his credit, took it in his stride, as did the other actors after their initial shock.

Then the interval arrived and one of our party, a lady of a certain age, appeared after a trip to the bar, to announce, raging, that the bar had no Diamond White. She then disappeared for about five minutes and returned with some Diamond White and two bottles of vodka. She had left with less than two pounds, as she couldn't afford a drink at the bar. I'd bought her one, and she poured about a third of one of the bottles of vodka into it and sclaffed it.

After the show we went round to meet the actors, who were terrific and warmly welcoming, and she appeared with yet more vodka. It was one of the best after-show parties I have ever been at.

On the bus on the way back her man said to me, with enormous pride, "Hur, she could shoaplift in a kebab shoap."